For Hie —

another song and
dance about rowing

Chris

BONNIE BRAVE BOAT ROWERS

The heroes, seers and songsters of the Tyne

Christopher Dodd

authorHOUSE

AuthorHouse™ UK Ltd.
1663 Liberty Drive
Bloomington, IN 47403 USA
www.authorhouse.co.uk
Phone: 0800.197.4150

© 2014 Christopher Dodd. All rights reserved.

No part of this book may be reproduced, stored in a retrieval system, or transmitted by any means without the written permission of the author.

Published by AuthorHouse 03/15/2014

ISBN: 978-1-4918-9552-8 (sc)
ISBN: 978-1-4918-9553-5 (e)

This book is printed on acid-free paper and set in Warnock Pro.

Because of the dynamic nature of the Internet, any web addresses or links contained in this book may have changed since publication and may no longer be valid. The views expressed in this work are solely those of the author and do not necessarily reflect the views of the publisher, and the publisher hereby disclaims any responsibility for them.

COVER: John Warkup Swift's painting Bob Chambers and Bob Cooper race on the Tyne, September 1864 *(Tyne & Wear Archives & Museums)*

Contents

Author's note vii

1. The Scotswood Express 1

2. The eye to see and the hand to fashion................23

3. Pulling clivor on the coaly river 59

Bibliography..87

Index 91

Books by Christopher Dodd

Pieces of Eight

Water Boiling Aft

Battle of the Blues

The Story of World Rowing

Boating

The Oxford and Cambridge Boat Race

Henley Royal Regatta

Author's note

Bonnie Brave Boat Rowers began life in the early 1980s as a sample chapter for a book about the first hundred years of the Amateur Rowing Association (now British Rowing). The book died in the water. But when Roger Bean contacted the River & Rowing Museum in 2012 for information about a professional sculler named Jack Hopper whose boat he was intending to restore, out came the forgotten manuscript, and Bonnie Brave Boat Rowers is the result.

Since its first draft, much information about the past prowess of rowing and boat building on the Tyne has come to light. I have deliberately left the story's setting largely in the ambience of early 1980s, while bottoming out the background and history of this long-gone world of the northeast of England, made possible by several works published in the intervening thirty years that are set out in the bibliography.

Notable among these are social histories of English rowing by Eric Halladay and Neil Wigglesworth, David Clasper's account of his forbears, and Ian Whitehead's superb biography of James Renforth. Whitehead's The Sporting Tyne (accompanying his Gateshead exhibition of the same name) chronicles the lives of

Tyneside's rowing and boatbuilding heroes, including the Claspers, Chambers, Cooper and Renforth. Keith Gregson's work on the song writers and performers of Newcastle's music halls shows how the oarsmen's adventures were marked and honoured.

Thanks go to the late David Lunn-Rockliffe of the ARA for the original idea, to Ian Whitehead of Tyne and Wear Museums for his editing skills, to Tyne ARC for introducing me to their waters in the 1980s, to Paul Mainds and Eloise Chapman of the River & Rowing Museum and Roger Bean, David Clasper, Bill Miller, Philip Pearson and Thomas E. Weil for images and reminiscences.

Lastly, my hope is that this book will refresh the story of rowing in the northeast and encourage memoirs and artefacts to come out of hiding. Send your information and inquiries to the River & Rowing Museum at info@rrm.co.uk

Christopher Dodd, River & Rowing Museum, 2014

Christmas Handicap poster, 1891, spelling out the Conditions: 'Any Competitor entering falsely will be disqualified or put back at the option of the Handicappers. Competing Entries from a distance must be accompanied by a Copy of recent Performances.' *(Tyne Rowing Club)*

The Tyne Championship Course in about 1870

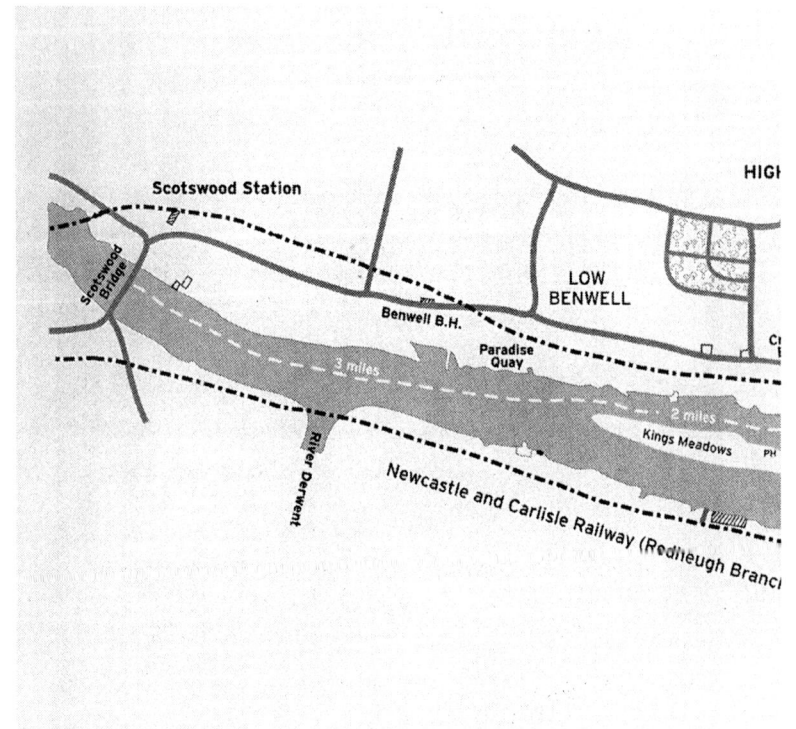

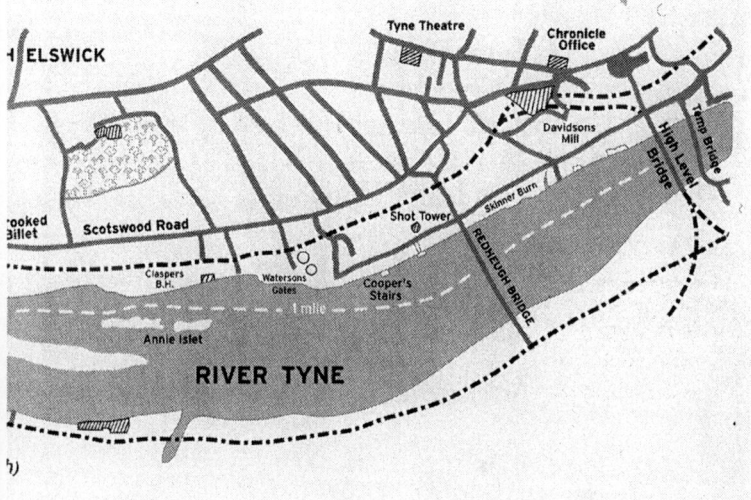

Christmas Handicap programme, 1908 *(Pearson Collection)*

1

The Scotswood Express

Every day for the three weeks before Christmas, Bill Hunter and Jack Briggs met Smith of Scotswood off the train from Hexham. They took him from Newcastle upon Tyne's Central Station down the steep banks to the riverside. He was forbidden to speak to anyone, save for a polite 'good morning'. His minders paid the boatman on his behalf for a half hour's sculling practice in one of Calder's boats, and the very first time he ventured out he almost didn't come back. The wash from a tug swept him against a collier at Dunston Basin, and the tug had to disengage its screw propeller to enable the sculler to escape. He never sculled in Dunston Basin again. When the day's work was done, Hunter and Briggs took his sculls for safekeeping and escorted him back to the Hexham train, paying for his ticket and making sure that he recognised some Hexhamite or other in the compartment in which he was to travel home. It wasn't just that their twenty-year-old charge had bad eyesight. They knew that a well-placed glancing hack on the ankle or a finger-crunching hand-shake could ruin their man's chances in the Christmas Handicap, and that Bill Chambers, one of Newcastle's biggest bookmakers and Smith's backer, would not be well pleased.

At home, boating from Hexham Amateur Rowing Club's wooden earth-floored shed on Tyne Green by the crystal bubbling waters of the upper, non-tidal river, Smith of Scotswood was just Jack Hopper, who'd come down to the club a couple of years beforehand and taught himself to scull. His elder brother Isaac was a bit of a sculler, too. Ned Bates, a pitman who was Jack's brother-in-law, gave him his first outing, after which he had been left to his own devices to make his mark among the sixty-odd members of the club. He received only one tip: 'That was to open my knees. Nearly every other professional kept the knees closed. When you come forward to take a pull, that knocks the wind out of ya. When you've got them slightly open your stomach goes into your knees a bit. That's the only professional hint I got—open your knees a few inches. I bought a book on sculling when I started. Supposed to be by a top-notcher. He was all wrong. When you feather, he reckoned to keep your blades on the water. The first regatta I was in, I was soaking wet with spray. I was told to get my hands down a bit. Water knocks the sculls out of your hands.'

That was how Hopper started, paddling about in the countryside in the clean Northumbrian air, protected from the wild Caledonian north by the closeness of Hadrian's Roman wall. He hung up his sculls when his boat was damaged in 1982, but when he was 20 in 1922 he was entered for his first Newcastle Handicap, under both his real and false names, to have a crack at the £100 prize. A hundred pounds was a lot of money in 1922. There would likely be 60 or 70 contenders, mostly men who toiled along the river or dug coal in the pits, but including a few well-known names among the professionals of rowing—maybe even a southerner or two, trying their chances from Christmas Day to New Year's Eve. It was two-by-two over half a mile, knockout, handicapped in seconds, and the draw made each evening. That was why Bill Chambers could not afford his find with a false name to say more than the bare civilities of the day; that is why word got around that Smith was a Yankee, and in other quarters that he was a Cockney; that is why he was not allowed to walk or travel in trains near folk who showed too much interest in his well-being, apart, that is, from the veteran scullers in the pocket of Chambers the bookmaker, Hunter and Briggs. That is why Smith's sculls and their dimensions had to be safeguarded from prying measurers and carpenters. And that is why Smith never practised his fast work in Newcastle. He made expeditions to Durham or Ebchester or far away from his own Hexham boathouse or his other club, the Hawthorn, which was downstream from the Swing Bridge in Newcastle, where he hardly ever ventured in any case.

A four approaches the High Level and Swing bridges, Newcastle upon Tyne *(David Clasper)*

Smith-Hopper was the fastest mover found by any bookie's runner in 1922. He was first spotted on August Bank Holiday Monday by someone hoofing his way from Hexham's railway station to the great Tyne Show. Hopper skimmed under the old stone bridge as the scout crossed it. Later the secretary at the Hawthorn club noticed Hopper put in a few strokes 'a bit sharp' at the end of a Sunday outing. Near the end of November he found himself undergoing a trial against Hunter at Hexham, with Briggs and Chambers looking on. They had come into the picture because a Scotswood man who had been working as a boat repairer at Hexham during the summer hire season had also spotted Hopper's talents and asked him that, if he ever thought of having a go at them, to let him know. In the trial Hopper was told to go from start to finish whether he was getting beat or not. After three strokes he was up. At the end his brother-in-law asked if they wanted to see Jack do a sprint start. No, the fella says, we've seen plenty. He told Hopper to report on Monday morning, took his sculls away with him, and Hopper became a 'keepers'.

He was kept for a month. So Smith was to scratch from the Handicap on 24 December or simply not show up for the draw, while the 20-year-old Hopper was to compete in his first Handicap before an immense crowd of Geordies in the city from where they took coals on Christmas Day in the morning. The races were held with the tide on a half-mile course from just above the High Level Bridge to just above Redheugh Bridge. So the scullers must be familiar with the water on the ebb and the flood. 'It was the worst course you could have picked on the Tyne,' Hopper says, 'through bridges which are not in line, shipping, strong tides, cold and foggy weather.'

John 'Nipper' Clark, who was chief boatman, says the same thing. 'The river was quite wide. You could lose your way if you were used to a narrow river. We knew where all the eddies was. After you leave Dunston and you come downstream and you catch the Redheugh Bridge, you've got a big buttment there and you come alongside the buttment, and as soon as you get off there's swirls boiling and you get farther over again, and if you get too far there you couldn't get back on the course again, 'cos the swell was coming that hard it'd shoot you straight to Newcastle. Oh, yes.'

Nipper, in the true Geordie way, pronounces Newcastle with a short 'a' and customarily finishes paragraphs of sentences with a quiet 'oh yes' as he remembers every detail. 'I could leave Dunston and come down through all the bridges'—including the Swing Bridge on which he used to work, downstream from the High Level—'I taught meself that much. I used to get [a sighting] on the gas yard chimneys that used to face the Redheugh Bridge. When I got on the Redheugh Bridge through there . . . that enabled you to get through the King Edward railway bridge if you watched that buttress, keep yourself off that way . . .

that's what used to beat a lot of them, oh yes. The tide's 14ft, nine o'clock tide's always the biggest. It's hard to know the course both ways. Spent me life on there.'

Nipper moves from side to side of his seat in the bar of the Commercial Hotel as he describes the course, re-living every stroke and seeing every landmark. He lives on the top floor of a tall block of flats not far from the centre of Gateshead, on the south bank of the Tyne looking across to Newcastle. Gateshead's civic buildings are set in a pleasant park on bluffs, surrounded by a concrete jungle of urban highways and close to apartment buildings which would have been better never born, ponging faintly of dampness and worse. From Nipper's windows you can see over the skyline of Gateshead towards the Tyne Valley's industrial and commercial landscape, much of it now derelict, stretching to the North Sea. Times are changing: the last handicap was in 1938 and Hitler's bombers put the kybosh on any postwar revival on the night of 3-4 April 1941 when they hit the Empire Club's boathouse which was situated near the High Level Bridge at the bottom of the Javel Group, a lane which ran down to the Tyne from the Close. Seventeen boats were destroyed.

Nipper was born in Gateshead, began coxing and paddling about in boats when he was eight years old, became a docker and then went to work on the Swing Bridge, which in the 1920s opened for up to 6,000 ships a year, mostly colliers, dirty British coasters with

Philip Pearson, winner of 1900 Christmas Handicap, with his coach and backers *(Pearson Collection)*

salt-caked smoke stacks, butting cargoes of Tyne coal through the North Sea in mad March days. Every winter he took six weeks off to run the boathouse and lovingly tend the boats for the Handicap. The boats, in Hopper and Clark's time, were supplied by Calder's Brewery, six identical shells named after winners of the Northumberland Plate at Gosforth races—*Guller, Carpathus, Double Hackle, Huntslaw, Irish Lake, Trestle*. Nipper Clark and Phil Adams, who used to do the Handicap's paperwork, can reel off their names. They can reel off the names of great scullers of the past, too. And Nipper used to lead an annual pilgrimage from the boathouse to repaint the railings at Renforth's memorial in Gateshead East cemetery. But more of Renforth by and by.

Nipper Clark and his mates ran a gym in Laski Street, Gateshead, in the converted hayloft of a coach house. The Brown brothers, gymnasts, were trainers. They built parallel bars, rings, all the equipment themselves. They couldn't afford to do otherwise. The lads from the iron foundries and glass works, from the hawser and paint and enamel factories, the lads who worked the quays and followed the fortunes of United, came to Nipper's gym. 'None smoked, drank, or courted,' he says. They took long jogs round Gateshead, where the population later flocked to the stadium whenever Steve Cram took on the best of the world. They scudded about on the river in sculling boats and fours. 'Weightlifting,' Nipper says, 'is ridiculous.' Most kept fit by their daily business of hard, manual work.

And Jack Hopper would agree. He would skip, cycle, exercise with a punch ball and a pair of spring dumbbells—'You go as slow as possible with them, one arm going up while the other goes down—and a little running, with some back and stomach exercises. 'I think big heavy weights are ridiculous,' he says, 'I was always fit. My job did it.' He started in the leather trade as a puller, using a block of wood about three feet high over which a sheepskin was stretched to pull the wool off the hide. 'The back and arms had it all the time.' It was piece work, so Hopper was hard at it, first in Hexham and later, after making his first appearance in the handicap, moving across the hills to Kendal in the Lake District, employed in a tannery until it closed in 1935. In Kendal he trained on a canal, rode his bike and built himself a contraption to simulate sculling using two 28lb weights in the little cellar of his house. When he moved to Carlisle in the engineering business he trained on Talkin Tarn, a circular lake in parkland east of Carlisle that has a tradition of rowing and an annual regatta on the first weekend of July.

But in 1922 all this was ahead of Jack Hopper. He was, temporarily, the property of a bookmaker. While he was masquerading as Smith of Scotswood in Newcastle, Nipper Clark and his likes were training scullers in Hexham. Nipper never trained scullers or crews on the Handicap course in case of spies. He used the Wear at Durham or Chester-Le-Street or the Tyne at Hexham for the real work. If his charges were sculling along by the Newcastle quays Nipper would tell them to sit on the side of the seat, so that they appeared incompetent. He would coach novices by sitting in the boat with them. 'I used to put a board over the back. I did all the movements and told them exactly what to do. Taught them by touch.' In the races he was never beaten off the mark, a darting lightweight who earned his nickname by beating the great Londoner Bert Barry, Doggett's Coat and Badge winner in 1925 and world champion in 1927, in the Handicap. He was christened John and born in 1913.

So, in the month of December the talent scouts, the bookies and the spies, the punters and the chancers roamed the river banks, strolled the quays, gathered in the pubs and clubs of an evening and a Sunday morning, particularly in the Anchor by the Swing Bridge, which was a rowers' pub where students held moots in the large first-floor room. The scullers came from the pits and the quays and the shipyards, from the hillsides of Northumberland and the flatlands of Durham, from the Wear and the Tees and the Scottish rivers, and sometimes from the Tyne's great rival river, the Thames. All along the Tyne were boathouses— Ryton, Blaydon, Scotswood, Dunston, the Northern at Gas Yard, the Empire at Gateshead, where Renforth used to row, St. Lawrence's, Tyne Main, Walker, Jarrow, South Shields, Tynemouth. The Empire Club, Newcastle, from where the Handicap was run, was thought to have connections with the Empire Theatre. Some were amateur, some were professional, or to be exact at that time, neither amateur nor professional under the confused state of the oarsmen's attempts at defining those terms that kept the rowing world split from the 1890s to the 1950s.

The carvel built boats were brought from Calder's cellar in to Nipper's charge. The earlier ones were 14in wide, the later ones 18in to accommodate the heaviest men. They had keels and scudded about in the wind if rowed by big men. If you could afford it, you were best off with two sets of blades, short ones to deal with caps or swell in really rough water, long ones for calmer conditions. Competitors gave Nipper 6d for 20 minutes practice each time they went off. Each time they came back, sewage had to be hosed off hulls, and boats were locked up at night, for many are the stories of shenanigans. They were inspected carefully before races. A rusty nail knocked casually into a keel could play havoc with a man's steering. A razor blade pressed into a seam could cause a boat to leak once it was out on the water. A toothpick slipped under the leather of a scull could throw a sculler's rhythm. A scull could snap at the first hard cut if a fretsaw had been at work on the loom. The handicappers studied previous performances and handicapped by lengths

Wilson Hepple: watercolour of King's Meadows Island with the Countess of Coventry pub and Armstrong's Elswick works *(Tyne & Wear Archives & Museums)*

until 1886, after which the allowances were made in seconds. This was applied at the start, so the scullers left the mark in succession with the less favoured competitor going first. The draw was done each evening, so that nobody could work out in advance whom they would meet in the next round. They tossed for boats. First out of the hat took the north bank, whichever way the tide was running.

Two steamboats followed the races, loaded with bookies and punters. Each competitor had a flagger with a megaphone in the bows of the steamer on his station who was engaged to bellow steering instructions. This presented another opportunity for cheating. And there were plenty of other hazards during the Christmas Handicap, like inexperience or ill luck in the face of wind, fog, tugs or shipping.

The conditions said that the handicap would be rowed strictly under Thames National Rules. 'The course upwards will be straight away from the starting boats, east of Davidson's jetty, finish the extra distance above Redheugh Bridge from north side. Down course to start opposite crane at the lead works to a point at east end of Herring's Timber Yard jetty. Any competitor rowing through the extreme channels of bridges will be disqualified. The men to be re-drawn for every tie. The men to toss for boats each heat. Any competitor failing to come forward when called upon for his heat will be disqualified. After the first man is started in each heat any competitor breaking away before he has received the word to go from the starter will be <u>disqualified</u>. ALL BYES MUST BE ROWED or rower will be disqualified.'

Scullers were admitted free on board the steamers to watch others race until they were themselves eliminated. In the 1920s tickets for the steamers cost two shillings for the morning or the afternoon races. The following was colossal. The local football team, Newcastle United, hadn't a look-in, according to Nipper. Banks were lined with onlookers, bridges were packed, and waterside pubs did a roaring trade.

Jack Hopper reached the semi-finals in 1922. On the way he learned some of the snags. When he won his first round tie the distance judge failed to fire the finishing gun, and the scullers could have raced all the way to Scotswood. Hopper then beat the red-hot favourite by the name of Whistle, a short man built like a side of ham, and Chambers lost interest in him. Hopper, who professes not to understand betting, reckons the reason was that Chambers had cleared his books, totalling £600, but he doubts the figure. It became clear to him later that Chambers was also backing a Scottish miner called Brownlee, a member of Walker and Wallsend Rowing Club, who was also still running.

Hopper met Mordue in his semi. They were on the 'up' course on the north side of the river with about eight feet of extra floodwater to cope with. Hopper had the worst station but learned, after being found guilty of a foul, that he had been on the wrong station all along because, after two names had been drawn for the first semi-final, the man making the draw had said 'That leaves Mordue and Hopper' when he should have said 'Hopper and Mordue'. Brownlee beat Mordue in the final.

In 1923 Hopper reached the semi-final again, this time backed by Hexham and Newcastle businessmen, and met T. Tonks of Walker and Wallsend, who was backed by Chambers. Hopper had to give Tonks two seconds off the start, and Tonks, the eventual winner of the Handicap, got three cuts at the water before Hopper got the word 'Go'. 'Three cuts in two seconds is just not possible,' he says.

In the following year Hopper acquired the tag of 'the world's unluckiest sculler' from the knowledgeable local pressmen who reported and interpreted the Handicap. The event was now worth £110, and the brewers Robinson & Anderson sponsored him. Again reaching the semi-final, he met T. English on the 'down' course, Hopper having one second. English's father was referee, and English stopped and claimed a foul when Hopper was drawing away on a bend. The referee stood down and asked Jack Dodds, a former winner from Hexham, to arbitrate. The scullers re-started, Hopper won, and Dodds gave the race to English. The newspapers all disagreed. English senior disassociated himself from the decision, the bookmakers declared all bets void. Dodds wrote to

Hopper offering to give him £100 to give to charity if anything dishonest could be proved against him. Hopper ignored the letter. He reckons that a gang aboard the steamer threatened Dodds.

In 1927 Hopper lost a semi-final for the fourth time. In 1933 he came back from his work in Kendal and reached the final for the first time. His opponent was Bert Barry of Putney whom he had beaten with seven seconds' start in 1924. This time he had 15 seconds against the man who had beaten Major Goodsell of the US for the world championship in 1927, and Barry knew he couldn't beat Hopper with a handicap like that. He told Hopper so. But Hopper's flagger failed him in the fog, and the Hexham man ran into the buttress of Redheugh Bridge, and Barry finished alone. And that, apart from a revival in 1938 run by the Empire and Gateshead & District clubs, was the last Newcastle Handicap.

The handicap fizzled out, lacking support, and Hitler's bombers cruelly scotched any thought of survival. The lack of support, Hopper says, stemmed from the way he was treated. There were seen to be too many wrong decisions, what with one thing and another. His epitaph, delivered in 1983, is: 'As regards professional racing, there's nothing honest about it, nothing at all.'

In his day Jack Hopper carried more money on his head than any other sculler in the handicaps. 'People knew I was honest and just put their money on me.

The start at the High Level Bridge *(David Clasper)*

But I never got anything out of it, only expenses. The only thing I got was when English beat me [on a foul awarded against Hopper]. The bookmakers wouldn't pay out, all bets were void, but they [gave me] £25 as a wedding present.'

'I've a good name on Tyneside,' he says. 'I was always straight. I never laid down for money. One fella offered me £10 once to make it easy for a chap. The year before I'd given him seven seconds start. "I know," he says, "but he's improved a lot." I gave him seven seconds and beat him. Next year he got into the final and fell overboard, so that was him finished . . . There's lots of things you could tell. I always pulled straight, as straight as I could. I didn't believe in washing down an opponent.'

After the demise of the Handicap Hopper continued to scull and race between his travels to the far west and the southwest—Lancaster in Lancashire and Nantwich in Cheshire—for his employer in the engineering business. 'I was noted for keeping the boat moving all the time. Most boats go in jerks. Mine went smoothly all the time. I never hurt myself rowing. Never got exhausted, like some of them. It's kept me right.'

He lives within a short walk of the rowing club at Hexham, and not far from the 12th century Abbey Church and its adjacent elegant market square. Some of his medals and trophies are in Hillside, near Newark, New Jersey, in the care of his daughter. The rest are about his neat cottage, including a model of a Handicap boat that he fashioned himself. It is just like the boats in which he raced and lost four semis and a final. Only the wheels of the sliding seat are not to scale, and the splashboards are a little too big, he says. Each rowlock is made out of a single piece of wire, and on winter evenings Jack Hopper polishes his boat with Cherry Blossom when he isn't encouraging youngsters down at the club.

And high in his tower in Gateshead, Nipper Clark has some models too. His are superb miniatures of a racing eight, four, oars and sculls in a big glass case with pride of place on the sideboard. Nipper didn't make these masterpieces of craftsmanship. He rescued them from the bar of the Anchor before they pulled down the rowers' pub. They're in good hands, and Nipper's keen eyes still scan the Tyne when anything is happening at the rowing clubs up and down stream. But his hydraulically operated Swing Bridge, 'quite simply a bucket of water,' seldom opens for a ship nowadays. And strollers on the quays would be surprised to see a sculling boat venture under the High Level.

The finish at Scotswood Suspension Bridge *(David Clasper)*

Sculling match on the Tyne between Hanlan and Boyd for the Championship of the World from The Graphic, 15 April 1882 *(River & Rowing Museum—gift of the British American Arts Association from the Collection of Thomas E Weil)*

2

The eye to see and the hand to fashion

Hopper's Hexham was termed 'The heart o'England' by its inhabitants because it stands midway between the North Sea and Solway Firth—and halfway between the English Channel and Pentland Firth. From the summit of the Abbey Church you can see where the two heads of the Tyne meet, the south Tyne from Allendale and the north Tyne from Tynedale. From the confluence the river follows pebbly shallows and rocky beds eastwards past Hexham and the Roman crossing point of Corbridge through a pastoral valley to ancient Ovingham Church where Thomas Bewick's memorial in the chancel says that his genius 'restored the art of engraving on wood'. Bewick taught himself to draw, using the church floor and the gravestones as canvas as well as his notebooks, and after apprenticeship to a Newcastle engraver became famous for his histories of quadrupeds and British birds.

Prudoe castle is across the bridge from Ovingham. And further east comes the Wylam cottage where

George Stephenson was born, the man who did more than most to change the world's communications by iron road. Then comes the tide stone, nineteen and a half miles from the sea, and Newburn on the north bank, where Tyne Amateur Rowing Club, founded in 1852, now has its boathouse. A stone head of the river god of Tyne is attached to its wall. The god has a three-plait beard surmounted by a basket of burning coals surrounded by emblems of trade—picks, shovels, fish, nets and wheat. It is after one of the nine masks depicting English rivers on the front of Somerset House in the Strand, London. The only other example in Newcastle is at the imposing Central railway station. Close by the south bank is the university's boathouse, near Ryton on the Blaydon side of the river.

This dazzling river was famous for salmon fisheries in the days before coal became the dominant industry of the Tyne. From Newburn and Blaydon the river is more of Clark than of Hopper. Its story is one of steelworks, of vast armament, shipbuilding and engineering factories set up by William Armstrong at Elswick, expanded by amalgamation with Joseph Whitworth and Co. all along the north bank at Scotswood. In the 1980s the company was owned by Vickers who constructed a huge new armaments factory on the Scotswood site to replace the old works at Elswick. The Tyne then flows along the quays of Newcastle and beneath the bluffs of Gateshead. From

Blyth RC, winners of the professional four-oared race at Durham Regatta in 1909 *(Pearson Collection)*

there to the bar at Tynemouth, where Nelson's trusty friend Admiral Collingwood looks out over the river he loved, the banks are solidly industrial, displaying all the wealth, hard work and engineering ingenuity of the people.

The reaches from Scotswood to the sea are, then, the Tyne of modern legend, of industrial revolution:

> *Tyne river, running rough or smooth,*
> *Brings bread to me and mine;*
> *Of all the rivers north or south*
> *There's none like coaly Tyne.*

And Newcastle is the base of it, has been since the Romans built their bridge there and established a defensive position as an important garrison point close to the end of their anti-Pict Hadrian's Wall, which runs 70 miles from the west coast to Wallsend, a little way east of Newcastle's old town. Newcastle was the first settlement along the Tyne to grow, dominating the economy of the area for hundreds of years, controlling—and often mismanaging—the river. The city grew jealous of its trade and its lifeline to the world. The burgers fought the bishops of Durham to the south for fishing and shipping rights, and for centuries prevented other settlements near to the sea from creating their own markets. All produce was required to be traded through Newcastle, and all colliers that carried coals to the Thames on the hazardous North Sea were required to return with a cargo of ballast and pay a fee to discharge it at the quays.

A great volume of this ballast ended up in the water or was dumped illegally at Tynemouth. Eventually this practice caused serious silting, and drastic measures had to be taken to save the Tyne as a navigable river and prevent Newcastle's commerce from choking. In his History of Newcastle upon Tyne, R. J. Charleton records that in Cromwell's time, Ralph Gardiner failed in an attempt to wrestle shipping from the taxing tyranny of Newcastle Corporation. During the mid-seventeenth century all ships and boats coming into the Tyne were compelled to sail upstream to Newcastle to unload their ballast and pay their dues, including those loading salt or coal at Shields, near the mouth of the river. Skippers risked shoals, rocks and sunken wrecks in the channel, and were often icebound in winter. The round trip from Shields to Newcastle is 20 miles and could take as much as two weeks. Only freemen of the city were allowed to pilot ships and only free carpenters of Newcastle were allowed to work on shipboard repairs. Fees were exorbitant.

The setting went unloved and unrecognized. The geographer Middleton summarized Newcastle in 1778 as ancient, large, disagreeable and dirty, but exceedingly populous and very rich—only 40 years after John Wesley, co-founder of the Methodist

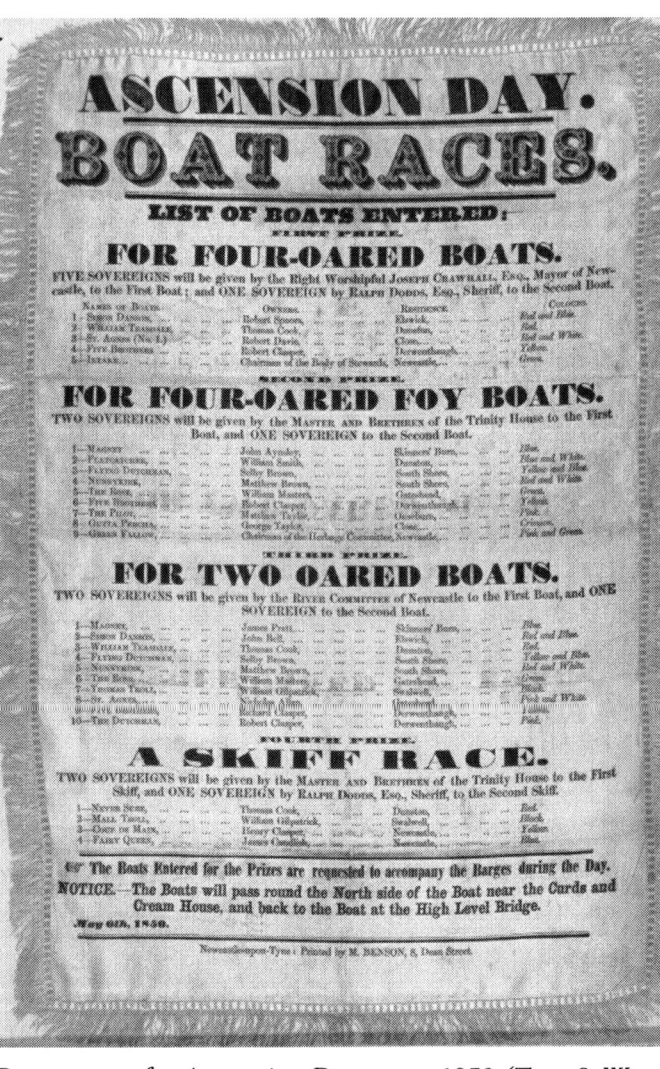

Programme for Ascension Day races, 1850 *(Tyne & Wear Archives & Museums)*

movement, said that were he not journeying toward heaven, he could not wish for a more pleasant abiding-place. By the end of that century an authority on nautical matters reported that ignorance, inattention and avarice—the corporation spent most of its revenue from the shipping business on improving the town rather than the river—had converted the Tyne to a 'cursed horse-pond'. A little later a surveyor engaged by ship owners reported that 'there was not water enough, when the tide was out, to cross in a sculler'.

Relief did not come until a reformed corporation began to make the river more navigable in 1836 to a plan drawn up by the engineer John Rennie after a campaign of ridicule against the authorities in the *Tyne Mercury* by 'Tim Tunbelly, Gent', who was really William Andrew Mitchell, editor of the *Newcastle Magazine*.

Improvements were slow to take effect, but eventually new quays, new docks, new drops for loading colliers downstream from Newcastle and dredgers all made their mark. Fishing fleets plied from North Shields. Lug-rigged foyboats, their solid black fenders alternating with white-painted sections of gunwale to create a checkered appearance, rowed or sailed out to sea off Sunderland to put pilots aboard ships to guide them into the Tyne. Having dropped its pilot, the foyboat was towed back to the Tyne so that its crew could moor the vessel. Barges, known as keels, plied the river, drifting with the tide and propelled by long sweep oars from the bows. When navigation improved, clinker-built Tyne wherries replaced keels. Shipbuilding and heavy engineering thrived as the nineteenth century drew to a close. Charleton's Victorian description is of a thrusting Tyne:

'For ten miles further the river flows . . . she is still beautiful here, bearing on her toil-stained breast the dark hulls of a mighty navy from the furthest ends of the earth, their white sails hanging pure and soft in the smoke-laden sky like the flash of the sea-gull's wing against the grey storm cloud, or with their tall, bare masts casting zigzag quivering reflections into her brown stream. She runs past iron works, which at night burn out ruddy and fierce, and flush her surface with blood-red streaks of light; and past chemical works, with their elevated chambers, that loom in misty mornings like lordly castles through the murky air. Past coal staiths, where the black wagons discharge their black loads into the dusky holds of black-hulled ships. Past chimneys innumerable, which belch forth their black smoke, blurring the face of the sky. Past ship yards, where the echoes are kept hard at work, answering the busy ringing hammers which close the iron sides of the growing monsters soon to be launched upon her tide . . . past quays where vessels lie in tiers, and where steam cranes puff and blow like fussy little giants at work.'

And despite the smoke and grimy buildings, says Charleton, no town in England is kept in cleaner condition. Each nook and corner is alive with reminiscence of old-world incident, memorials of munificence and people's enterprise, and picturesque groupings of architecture.

Charleton's vision has changed now. Newcastle has spread to Tynemouth on the north bank, and Gateshead has spread to South Shields on the south. Downtown Newcastle is in clean condition. The air is purer, the ways of industry changed, a landscape altered drastically by scars of development and decline in the means of production and transportation. The modern prestigious Civic Centre is a long way from the water. The river has taken a back seat in the economy of the area since the heydays of heavy engineering and shipbuilding in Victorian times, and since the bustling 1920s youth of Nipper Clark and Jack Hopper. No longer would Nipper have to hose the sewage from the bottom of a Handicap boat, and seals sometimes accompany scullers at Newburn on their outings upstream. The warehouses along the quays are finding refurbished uses as offices, restaurants and pubs. There is a thriving Sunday market. The Custom House and the Guildhall, the old fish market, the Mansion House and the Keelmen's Hospital are situated on or close to this waterfront, together with merchants' houses. Behind them the city is piled high, reached by alleys and closes and tortuous steps and inclines, with the remains of the castle on the nearest bluff to the river, and the delicate arches supporting the crown and spire of the cathedral church of St. Nicholas, a light visual touch if you can get a glimpse through the more recent palaces of commerce.

And the bridges, all but one high above the river, add to the drama of the setting. To awake on a sleeper from the south as the train pulls across the High Level on a misty morning is an exciting vision for the stranger, a chasm for the river opening suddenly beneath the moving window, with no hint of what is to come.

Until the pedestrian tunnel (1951), the road tunnel (1967) linking Jarrow on the south side with Willington Quay and the 'Blinking Eye' Gateshead Millennium pedestrian bridge (2001), the bridges were the only river crossings, except for ferries, between the city and the coast. There are six of them near the core of the place now. Sailing downstream, the Redheugh comes first, a brand new replacement for the bridge of 1901 that replaced another which carried gas and water mains across the river from 1870. Then comes the old North Eastern Railway Company's King Edward Bridge, opened in 1906, and then the elegant concrete span of the Metro Bridge opened in 1981 for the rapid transit system that has revolutionized public transport on Tyneside. Then comes the spectacular High Level Bridge, finished in 1849, with an upper tier for rail traffic and a lower for road, engineered

The eye to see and the hand to fashion

by Thomas Harrison and Robert Stephenson, son of railway engineer George. They used an estimated 5050 tons of iron, supplied by Hawks, Crawshay and Sons of Gateshead. The boat builder and oarsman Harry Clasper, of whom more later, once worked for this company and married into the Hawks family. His uncle Ned rowed in some of his crews. The arches are each 124ft 10in in span and the parapet of the railway is 132ft 6ins from the bed of the river.

Then comes the low level Swing Bridge, where Nipper Clark used to work, on the site of the Roman bridge, designed by Armstrong in 1876 to replace a stone one that restricted shipping. The new structure afforded access upstream to Elswick and Scotswood and Dunston for much larger vessels than previously. And last but not least, the Tyne Bridge, a massive impression dominating the Victorian office blocks nearby, opened in 1928. It carries the principal road from Gateshead, is of the two hinged-arch type, and is of similar design to Sydney Harbour Bridge in Australia, though less than a third of the size. A myth has grown up that Tyne Bridge was the prototype for Sydney, but the facts are that Sydney was designed in 1916 and construction began in 1923 and was completed in 1932, whereas work on Tyne Bridge began in 1925 and was completed in three years. The two bridges did share a builder, however— Dorman Long of Middlesbrough (the Long family had connections with London RC in the nineteenth century).

Beneath these structures and along miles of banks and docks and creeks, through the age when sail power gave way to steam power and then to diesel, indeed right into modern times, men built and worked wooden boats to service the bigger fry on the Tyne. Men like George Dunn, a master shipwright who had a wonderful physique and drank dark brown ale copiously, remembered by Nipper Clark and Phil Adams. He repaired barges when he ran out of beer money. 'He would go home and get up at 3 a.m. to dismantle a wherry,' Nipper says. 'He knew the tide. He'd renew planking and caulking, at night, any time. He'd hands of iron, a genius. He'd have been a millionaire if he'd kept off the pop.'

In plotting the Tyne as a rowing man's river, the challenges and the skills come from shipwrights and ferrymen, foyboatmen and keelmen, pitmen and builders of working boats who then looked to the water for recreation and races. And it is worth reiterating that this activity was about more than rowing. It was about money. Regattas charged entry fees. Match racers had to raise part of the stake, either themselves or through promoters and backers. Side bets were big business, and large cash prizes were on offer. Ian Whitehead's crude calculation is that the average weekly unskilled wage on Tyneside in 1870 was £1 a week. Multiply by more than 200 for an

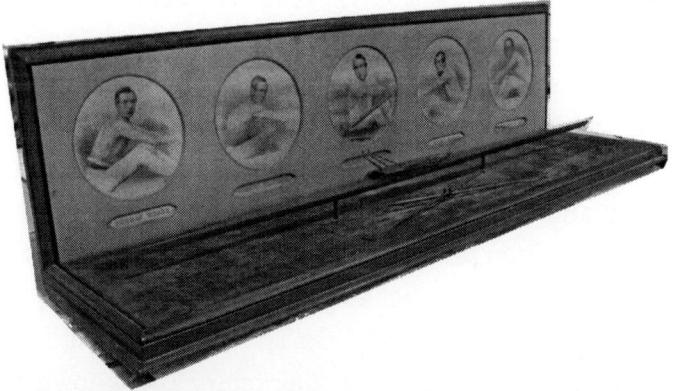

Model of sculling boat 'James Renforth', possibly Clasper made, with portraits of Thomas Hoare, Bob Chambers, Harry and John Hawks Clasper and Henry Kelley *(River & Rowing Museum)*

equivalent sum in the twenty-first century, and you can see why a £50 handicap was worth competing for.

Since the first of August 1821, Battle of the Nile day, when a North Shields boat, *Experiment*, specially designed for racing was awarded first prize at a competition to mark George IV's accession to the throne, Geordies raced in handicaps and took side bets, organised regattas from the Tyne bar to Hexham, made summer trips to Chester-le-Street, South Hylton, Blyth Cambois and Talkin Tarn, to Ebchester where the water confined races to two-by-two out-and-back round a stake with the result usually turning on the turn, and Corbridge where crockery and cutlery sets were common prizes (the boathouse at Corbridge and its contents were swept away in the great flood of 1955 that altered the river bed and spoilt a good stretch of rowing water). Ascension Day races, also known as Barge Day, began on the Tyne in 1830 and became part of a festival that included horse racing on King's Meadows Island, which is now an island no more. By the way, the *Experiment's* achievement was not what it may sound. The revolutionary boat did not appear in the race because the other crews objected to a specially designed boat taking part. *Laurel Leaf* won, but *Experiment* was given the prize.

Professional rowing on the Tyne could be said to start here, and much influence on the more commonly known roots of rowing came from the competitiveness, ingenuity and in some cases pure genius of these Geordies. For the forerunners of the Hoppers and Clarks produced technical developments in racing boat design that transformed the sport and had profound effect on the better known events such as the Oxford and Cambridge Boat Race, Henley Royal Regatta and the world professional championship races. In the mid-nineteenth century, when rowing was the sport with the widest following in England, Tynesiders such as Jewitt, Clasper, Taylor, Swaddle and Winship etched their names into the history of racing boat design. Chambers, Renforth and a host of others made names for themselves as professional competitors in places far away from Newcastle, and received heroes' acclamation, decent burials, and lasting memorials when they came home.

Four developments combined to transform the ship's boat from a tub to a sleek racing shell—the outrigger, the swivel, the sliding seat and the abolition, or at least the bringing inboard, of the keel. Matthew Taylor of Ouseburn has gone down in history as introducing the keel-less boat. A ship's carpenter at work on the *Himalaya*, he was engaged by Royal Chester Rowing Club as trainer in 1854, for £2:5s a week. During that year he built an outrigger fixed-seat four, the *Victoria*, which had a smooth bottom. He achieved this by using carvel construction in which planks are fitted flush together instead of overlapping, and taking the keel inboard. In 1855 the Chester crew used it to win the Stewards' Challenge Cup at Henley

Royal Regatta. Next year Taylor built an eight in which Chester won both the Grand and the Ladies' Plate at Henley.

Oxford's president for the 1857 Boat Race, A. P. Lonsdale, promptly engaged Taylor to build a boat for Oxford University Boat Club. Lonsdale paid for it from his own pocket because nobody else at Oxford showed any enthusiasm for the idea. His crew used it to beat Cambridge by more than half a minute from Putney to Mortlake, having engaged Taylor 'not to instruct us in the art of rowing'—professional coaching being banned in the Boat Race—'but to show us the proper way to send his boat along as quickly as possible'. The original Chester eight, meanwhile, was sold to Exeter College, Oxford, who used it to go head of the river in the 1857 bumping races and to win the Ladies' Plate. The future Eton coach Edmond Warre was rowing in the 1857 Oxford boat. His Eton crews won the Ladies' six times between 1864 and 1870 in a similar craft.

Taylor also built the boat that Cambridge used to win the 1858 Boat Race, and he went on to make more boats for Oxford, Eton and Chester. His hulls were regarded as very modern. His 55ft. eights were some ten feet shorter than keeled eights in use at the time. The greatest beam was 25 inches and was positioned well forward, and by these means both the skin friction and the weight of the craft were reduced. His original Chester four, the *Victoria*, is at the River & Rowing Museum at Henley.

Taylor spent many years himself competing as a sculler. On New Year's Day in 1851, for example, he raced William Patterson of Skinnerburn for £5 on the Tyne. Taylor fouled Patterson, Patterson fouled Taylor and was awarded the race, 'thus terminating what aquatic brethren thought would be a tight buckle'. Taylor's designs introduced a new element and skill into boat racing, for his keel-less shells were difficult to balance. His experience of seventy races on a dozen rivers taught him to teach oarsmen to feather low in calm water, and to get hold of the water at the beginning of the stroke with a great wrench. This was not to the taste of onlookers at first, but appeared to be a step in the right direction for handling the sleeker and lighter boats.

According to W. B. Coventry in his book The Racing Eight, published in 1922, Taylor solved the problem of skin surface resistance for fixed seat boats with remarkable accuracy. Coventry wrote for the expressed purpose of demonstrating the mechanical principles affecting the speed of racing eights, and to show that the application of these principles 'satisfactorily explains the remarkable success of the boats that were built by Matt Taylor more than 60 years ago'. He attributed the prejudice shown against the Taylor boats to the little general understanding, in the 1850s, of the relationships between the shape of hulls and their skin resistance, known as wetted surface. 'With a given displacement, the shorter the boat and

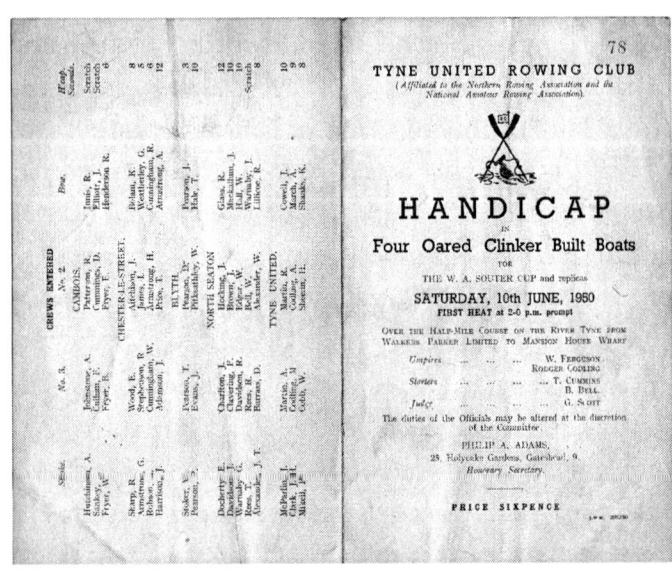

Programme for four oared clinker built handicap, 1950
(Pearson Collection)

the greater the draught, the smaller is the resistance,' Coventry says. The development of the sliding seat in the 1870s made the calculations different. But the Newcastle men of this time, Coventry pointed out, were superb oarsmen.

Thus Taylor made his mark, but it is far from certain that he was the first builder of a keel-less boat. The design, as distinct from the construction, of the first Taylor boats at Royal Chester has been claimed for J. B. Littledale who was the club's captain, stroke, and benefactor. Indeed, Gilbert Bourne alleged that Littledale attempted to adapt the lines of the Great Eastern to a racing boat. It is certainly true that he worked in close cooperation with the Ouseburn boat builder. The boat builders of the day worked independently of clients and oarsmen at their peril.

Several authorities cite Harry Clasper as the first builder of keel-less boats. Sir Theodore Cook, writing in Rowing at Henley (1919), says 'the keel-less hull which Harry Clasper used for his cedar skiff when he raced Robert Coombes on the Tyne in 1844 was in fact the prototype of the boats which Matt Taylor so enormously improved', and he quotes a letter from Harry's son Jack claiming that Harry was the inventor and user of smooth-bottomed boats long before Taylor was heard of. 'I steered my father and his crew at the Thames Regatta of 1849, and he used the same smooth-bottomed boats as are in use now,' wrote Jack Clasper to Cook. Robert Jewitt also put in a claim in a dispute with Clasper in a newspaper, alleging that in 1843 he was the first to use one strake from keel to gunwale. C. M. Pitman says in his Record of the University Boat Race (1909) that the first keel-less four was built by Harry Clasper in 1847, and used by Oxford to win the Stewards' Cup in 1852.

Clasper was born at Dunston-on-the-Tyne in 1812. His parents moved to Jarrow and he worked in the pits as a lad, but returned to the Dunston area in his teens and was employed as a cinder burner at the coke ovens of Garsfield Coke Co., thence becoming a wherryman for the same company when he was about twenty. He eventually lived at Derwenthaugh, a hamlet on the south bank of the Tyne where the Derwent flows into it, opposite Scotswood on the north bank.

He and his five brothers—Robert, William, John, Richard and Edward—all involved themselves with aquatics. Both William and John drowned while indulging in it. Harry himself became a celebrated champion sculler in the 1850s, and crews of Clasper brothers became notorious. Witness a report of Durham regatta in 1860:

'The first heat [for the Patron's Plate] was between the Claspers and Newby's crew and was claimed by the latter on a foul which was decided against them by the stewards. This enraged the Durham populace and the final heat between the Claspers and the Taylors could not take place in consequence of some foolish and ill-judged Durham men pelting the Claspers with stones from the banks.'

Earlier, Harry's son Jack had been involved in a sculling match:

'On the boats starting Robinson endeavoured to pull right into Clasper's boat, but missing it the oars became entangled, when the former jumped out of his boat and tried to pull the latter out of his. Clasper, seeing that all chance of winning the race was gone, and that his boat was likely to be capsized in the struggle, hit Robinson on the head with his fist, and was just on the point of striking him with his oar when he found that his boat was fast filling with water and going down foremost, and to save himself he had to jump out and swim for the shore . . .'

When Harry first formed a crew there was no such thing as a racing boat—at least, not on Tyneside. All boats doubled as ferries for people and goods. But he set out to fine down their unwieldy design by shedding weight and changing the shape of hulls to produce a boat for racing that would afford a crew the best possible leverage through the water. His ideas came to a head as early as 1842, when he and his brothers were beaten from Tyne Bridge to Lemington by Coombes's crew from London for £300. The Claspers used *St Agnes*, built by John Dobson of Hillgate, Gateshead, and described as 'a beautiful model of this class of running boat' but, at 160lbs, heavier than Coombes's boat, which was wider at

40ins to *St Agnes's* 29ins, but speedy nevertheless. Both were rowed off the gunwale, meaning that they didn't have outriggers.

St Agnes was clinker, like the Thames boat; Harry was already at work on the *The Five Brothers*, a 37ft five-strake mahogany craft with an inboard keel, smooth bottom and iron outriggers, two feet wide at the widest point. Her hull was French polished instead of black leaded and greased. She was ready for Tyne Regatta in August 1843 when a crew of Claspers won a purse of £525, and Harry also won the scullers' race. Later that year they lost one and gained two victories on the Tyne. In June next year, with his wife's uncle Ned Hawks in the crew, Clasper took *The Five Brothers* to the Thames and won a £50 prize while narrowly missing the Champion Fours (£100).

The new boat was much lighter than *St Agnes* but heavier than the Thames boats. The *Almanack* reported that 'she created much speculation and excitement among the Thames watermen. Her construction was quite revolutionary to their settled notions of racing vessels, and it was believed it would be impossible to row her steadily, as she was as round in the bottom as the section of half a gun barrel.'

In December 1844 Harry built a sculling boat for his losing race against Coombes on the Tyne. Was it keel-less? It was described in the *Newcastle Weekly Journal* as 'a perfect model in form, almost a toy, more fit as an ornament for a parlour than a boat to row

Blyth RC at the Golden Fleece, 1900 *(Pearson Collection)*

in', derivative from 'the beau ideal of his four-oared gig'. It weighed 49lbs to Coombes's 43lbs, so the boats must have been similar while the southerners' paring down of traditional Thames boats continued to lead in weight reduction. It is, therefore, highly probable that both were keel-less. There is a theory that Coombes's boat was built by William Pocock, whose line was to become boat builders to Eton and to America.

In 1845 Clasper returned to the Thames Regatta with another four-oared boat, the *Lord Ravensworth*, which was a further improvement on *The Five Brothers* (in which the brothers won Newcastle's Barge Thursday gala race for several years). The crew consisted of Harry at stroke, brothers William and Robert with uncle Ned, and brother Richard as cox. On this occasion they won the Champion Fours, beating two other crews, and were given the title of world champions for four-oars. A hero's welcome greeted their return to Newcastle, where Clasper sold the *Lord Ravensworth* for £80.

The first outrigger—the first, that is, after the demise of galleys—appeared in 1828, according to Robert S. Hunter's 'Rowing in Canada since 1848'. The claim goes to Anthony Brown of Ouseburn who had his boat builder Ripley fix wooden blocks to the side of *The Diamond* to race *The Fly* of Scotswood. In the same year Frank Emmett of Dent's Hole tried outriggers and in 1830 he fitted iron riggers to *The Eagle*—a year in which he accompanied Count

István Széchenyi in a row from Pest to the Black Sea in the *Juliette*. Wager wherry boats appeared in the 1830s, narrow in beam clinkers with flared sides for rowlocks, weighing as extraordinarily little as 25lbs. In America, George Steers built an outrigged coxed four in 1838 weighing only 140lbs and drawing only four inches of water. He moved on to become a famous naval architect, designing the schooner *America* for Commodore John C. Stevens that in 1851 defeated a fast 100-ton British yacht *Titania* over a 40-mile out-and-return course off Cowes. *Titania's* owner was Robert Stephenson who designed the High Level Bridge across the Tyne at Newcastle; the cup carried off to New York became the America's Cup.

In the 1840s Harry Clasper set about improving the attempts of Brown, Emmett and Steers. He fitted iron outriggers to a four on the Tyne in 1845, and outrigged boats became more common in the North, particularly in Durham, than in the South, although they were also evident in Dublin at the time. But Clasper wasn't the only one. Experiments took place relatively frequently. Oxford used a carvel-built keel-less boat in their race against Cambridge in 1841, but lost. Next year Cambridge reportedly had an outrigger built in eight days, but didn't use it. In 1844 the professional sculler Robert Newell beat four Belgians in a gig from Ostend to Bruges. Newell was in a boat belonging to Captain Tollemack and built by

Blyth RC, winners of Durham professional handicap off scratch, 1929. Left to right: Cox Pip Pearson, J Short, H Fulcher, J Fulcher, Bob Pearson *(Pearson Collection)*

Wentzell and Cownden of Lambeth that stunned the Belgians for her 'lightness and beauty of construction'.

In the same year Dr. Furnivall of Trinity Hall and Jack Beesley of St John's, Cambridge, claimed the first two narrow wager boats, and Samuel Wolsencroft of Civil Engineers College attempted to construct an outrigged sculling boat with a skin from a single piece of wood, without success. Another unsuccessful experiment took place in North Shields in 1845 when some brewery men tried a two-oared skiff of tin with air boxes in it.

J. W. Conant of St John's College, Oxford, went to Henley in an outrigger in 1845 and survived for one round of the Diamond Sculls against T. B. Bumsted who was in a wager wherry. Conant made his mark: 'In a few strokes Mr. Conant led by over a length, showing in an extraordinary manner the superiority of the outrigging boat over the others ... Mr. Bumsted fairly turned round on his thwart to see what had become of Mr. Conant.' All the stranger, then, that Conant lost the three-boat final badly, causing the Henley recorder to speculate that both Wallace and Chapman may have been in outriggers. Pity he didn't take a look.

By this time, partly outrigged gigs in which the stroke and bow seats had riggers were in evidence, and the outrigger breakthrough came in 1846 when both Oxford and Cambridge used them in the Boat Race. So by the mid-1840s the young Clasper had taken this important contribution to the narrowing and lightening of hulls to a state reliable enough to be used by crews seeking success. Oxford won the Stewards' at Henley in a Clasper four in 1852. Talkin Tarn were using a keel-less Clasper four and Tyne Amateur RC a similar Jewitt boat in 1853. Similar developments were taking place in America. James McKay, an Englishman working in Portland, Maine, and then St. John, New Brunswick, made two boats for Harvard in 1857, a 51ft lapstreak coxless eight and a coxless six christened *Harvard*. Outriggers were in evidence, Yale managing to pull five of them off their boat in three days of practice in 1859.

Oars were under scrutiny as well. Early oars were heavy, square-loomed, weighted with lead at the handle, with long straight blades and of different lengths. Scooped blades appeared on the Thames by the 1840s. Harry Clasper produced oars with scooped blades and round looms in the 1850s, known as the Newcastle oar. Oars of light spruce instead of heavy ash appeared in America in 1855. In the 1880s other shapes—'coffins' and 'barrels'—were being tried. In 1887 Aylings of Putney produced a brass holder for the leather to address the weak point where the leather was nailed to the loom. Tubular and girder oars were produced before the First World War. Clasper's son, John Hawks Clasper (known as Jack), solved the problem of steering cambered boats when he designed a fin for James Taylor's boat in 1870 (R.

A. W. Green had tried a cambered, cigar-shaped boat in 1863). Caius College, Cambridge, fitted tubular steel outriggers to their boat in 1891, borrowing new technology from the bicycle frame.

The men of Tyne do not have first claim on the other technical innovations, the sliding seat or the swivel oarlock to replace fixed thole pins on an outrigger. The first reported design of slides was in Chicago in 1857, while swivels became popular only in the twentieth century, and the development of the slide and how to use it—progression from sliding *on* a seat to sliding *with* a seat—was the main spur. John Babcock of Nassau Boat Club, New York, was experimenting with sliding in the 1850s and was probably the first to construct a reliable slide, although Herbert Manchester's Four Centuries of Sport in America (1931) attributes the invention to the American professional sculler Walter Brown in 1861. In 1869 Brown was staying at the Ord Arms Inn, Scotswood, for his race against the Thames professional William Sadler on the Tyne. James Taylor's four who were experimenting with sliding prior to taking on the best of Canada were also based at the Ord Arms, and it is inconceivable, says Eric Halladay in Rowing in England, that they would not have compared notes. When Taylor returned from Canada in 1871 he fitted two sculling boats with bone runners in steel grooves, and then gave his four the same treatment. This caught the eye when visiting the Thames and led to Francis Stepney Gulston's experiments with slides at London Rowing Club (Thames RC followed suit, ordering an eight with slides from Jewitt of Dunston in 1871-72).

Other sources give Babcock the credit for this most important of innovations in 1870. His slide consisted of a ten-inch wooden frame covered with leather and grooved at the edges. This sat on two brass tracks up to a foot long lubricated with lard, giving the oarsman a sliding action of about six inches. In the same year, Yale appeared for their match with Harvard on genuine slides—seats moving on greased slides—made by Brown, who was now their coach. Harvard used greased seats. Grease reportedly spread everywhere around the Yale boat's new gadget, while Harvard's way was exhausting, to say the least.

Many had tried to slide by greasing the seat with lard or tallow, or in the case of H. A. Freeman, topping the seat with a sheet of plate glass. Tyneside men, including Claspers, Chambers, Renforth and Fawcus slid for spurting purposes, and Harry induced his pupil John Goldie of Lady Margaret to use olive oil in the Diamond Sculls in 1871 (Goldie lost to Fawcus). Tom Winship, another Tyne professional, coached the Lancaster club John O'Gaunt to slide on grease over the entire Henley course in 1870, to disastrous effect.

The first appearance of slides at yardstick British rowing events was in 1872 (London RC at Henley) and 1873 (Boat Race). And it is worth noting again that Babcock's successful innovation threatened Matt Taylor's notions of hull shape because the slide required larger staterooms for the oarsmen, and therefore lengthier boats. Taylor did good work for his time. 'At the job of combining the practical skill of the watermen with the mental intelligence of the amateur,' wrote A. A. Casamajor, the celebrated London amateur sculler in the *Field* in 1858, 'Matthew Taylor had no equal among amateurs.' Walter Bradfield Woodgate, writing in 1888, remarked that 'as to shapes of hull, the earliest Mat Taylor boats have never been surpassed, and were much faster than modern builds.'

Woodgate identifies Taylor's peculiarity as putting his greatest beam well forward instead of amidships, and not adhering to the principle of seating all oarsmen at equal distance from one another, so reducing his beam and depth aft. 'Builders of the present day construct as if the only problem which they had to solve was to force a hole through the water in front of the boat . . . a racing boat leaves a vacuum behind her, and until that vacuum is filled she is sucked back into that vacuum . . . the problem to be solved in designing the lines of a boat is so to arrange her entry into the water that what she displaces in front may with greatest ease flow aft to fill the vacuum aft which she leaves as she progresses.' They said, Woodgate says, that Taylor built by rule of thumb. 'So, perhaps he did, but his builds have never been surpassed.' His reputation came from hulls, not from slides.

Sir Theodore Cook, in writing about the Thames boat builder George Sims, said: 'As he did it, the thing savoured of Turner's notion of perspective, a realization of what should be, without any knowledge of what must be. There was that strange sympathy in the boat builder which was in Matt Taylor, and the Claspers too, and which is outside all calculation.' They possessed the accuracy of the eye to see and of the hand to fashion exactly what they had in their minds. Other Tyneside boat builders, notably Jewitt, Swaddle and Winship, came to make their marks in the wider world of crafting delicate oar-powered machines. London Rowing Club, for example, founded in 1856 and the pioneer of rowing for amateurs on the professionals' Championship Course at Putney, ordered its first new boats from Jewitt, a relationship fuelled by lively correspondence concerning design and specification that took place over several years.

The cleverness of the northeastern boat builders made their names famous throughout the land, whilst Harry Clasper became a hero on Tyneside. At his testimonial dinner in 1866 at the Cumberland Arms his health was proposed as the 'father and teacher of modern aquatics, and there was no man in England to whom the present style of boat rowing was more indebted than to him. The name of Clasper was known and spoken of with respect and admiration upon the Scottish hills, the rivers on the Continent, in the lobby of the House of Commons, the class rooms of universities, the literary clubs, the halls of aristocracy, and the cottage of the artisan'.

Clasper, in reply, said that 'if a man honestly and fairly rowed on the Tyne he would find people willing to support and back him'. Mr. Pringle claimed in his speech that 'the London watermen at first laughed at his boat, but after the race they quickly copied it, and now the lines of Harry's skiff have been adapted to sea-going clipper ships and screw steamers'. Enough was raised at the dinner to buy Clasper an off-licence, and he later moved to the Tunnel Inn, North Shore, where he died of 'congestion of the brain' in 1870. Ian Whitehead proclaims him a true hero of rowing in his book The Sporting Tyne: 'Harry Clasper was a great oarsman, boat designer and builder: he was a very successful stroke oar, a superb team leader, a good sculler and highly skilled coach.' Whitehead quotes the wisdom of Clasper the coach:

'A trainer must always exercise a wise discretion, and it is folly to attempt to train a man by any set of rules. Some men who are not in good condition require good feeding and moderate work to bring them up to the mark. The work in short must be regulated according to the constitution and habits of the man, and the food, to a certain extent, must be adopted in a similar manner.'

Bob Bagnall's original sliding seat, 1871 *(Tyne & Wear Archives & Museums)*

Harry could also be pig-headed, difficult and stubborn, and his all-round abilities stopped short of being a good publican. Harry now stands, handsome and magnificent in stone effigy, overlooking the Tyne where he learned his skills and set up his triumphs, in the cemetery of Whickham parish church, set on a hill to the southwest of Derwenthaugh.

It is a beautiful place, a leafy retreat from the industry in the valley close by, and Clasper's sculptor, George Burn, gave him a canopy over his head embellished with flowers on stone pillars with Romanesque capitals, the motif being aquatic plants and boat builders' ephemera. On the base is carved:

> 'Beneath this monument, reared to his memory, by the ardent affection of friends and admirers from every class, and from all parts of the kingdom, and in this sacred spot commanding a full view of that noble river, the well-loved scene of former triumphs, rest the mortal remains of Henry (Harry) Clasper, the accomplished oarsman and boat builder of Derwenthaugh who died July 12 1870, aged 58 years. 'Know ye not that they which ran in a race run all, but one receiveth the prize, so run that ye may obtain.'

Clasper's widow, his daughter Dorothy and his two sons Jack and Henry moved to Putney, where they set up in boat building, and Jack inherited the abilities of his father.

Meanwhile, others were to make a song and a dance to spread the fame of Geordie scullers and oarsmen, and to earn their memorials.

3

Pulling clivor on the coaly river

One neet, when walkin doon the Kee,
Aw heard a yung lass singing,
The cheerful soond she sent a'roond,
Wi' voice byeth clear an' ringin,—
"Me lad's away, but cum when he may
He'll not find me cumplainin,
For hoo can he cum eftor me
The time that he's i'trainin?"
　—Me Bonny Brave Boat Rower, to the tune of 'Martha, the Milkman's Daughter'.

The Christmas Handicap, first run in 1876, was not the only sculling event on the Tyne, and half a mile through the bridges was not the only course. Races were held frequently from the High Level Bridge (1849) upstream to Scotswood Chain Bridge (1831), a distance of three and a half miles. This was known as the Championship course. Races of one and a half or two miles finished between the north bank and King's

Cabinet photograph of the Tyne Crew taken a few days before the race in which Renforth collapsed and died, showing Renforth, Kelley, Chambers, Percy and Bright (spare man). Photographed by William Notman of Montreal. 20 August 1871 (*River & Rowing Museum—gift of the British American Arts Association from the Collection of Thomas E Weil*)

Meadow Island where there was an ideally situated pub, the Countess of Coventry.

When Harry Clasper raced Robert Newell in 1846, five specials followed on the Newcastle to Carlisle line. Tens of thousands witnessed Clasper's defeat by the Londoner, and the *Times* reported that 'the race terminated without a solitary cheer, the banks of coaly Tyne were dumb, enormous sums of money will have been won and lost'. An agricultural merchant records seeing Robert Cooper beat James Taylor for £100 on 12 April 1869, and attending three important races in November of the same year. On the eighteenth a Tyne four beat a London four; on the nineteenth the American sculler Walter Brown, claimant to the invention of the sliding seat, beat the Londoner William Sadler; on the twentieth, a Saturday, James Renforth and Taylor of the Tyne lost to Harry Kelley and Joseph Sadler from the London crew in double sculls. Railway companies organized excursions for fans to attend races, and spectator trains from Newcastle on the north bank and Redheugh on the south would follow races, both lines affording a bird's-eye view of the river for most of the way to Scotswood. Trainers sometimes coached by train, giving their men a set time to start rowing to coincide with the departure of a Scotswood puffer that would serve as pacemaker for sculler and transport for timekeeper.

Rowing became immensely popular in the 1840s, peaked in the 1860s with the professionals dominating the scene, and began to loose its pull twenty years later. Challenges for the world professional sculling championship were held three times on the Tyne: in 1866 Kelley of Fulham, London, beat James Hammill of Pittsburg, USA, over 4.5 miles on Independence Day, 4 July, and again in a five-mile contest with a turn next day. A year later Kelley retained his title by beating the former ironworker 'Honest Bob' Chambers of St. Anthony's, Newcastle. In 1882 the Canadian champion Ned Hanlan beat Robert Boyd of Middlesbrough from the Mansion House to Scotswood Bridge.

Matches for the championship of England, which sometimes ran concurrently with the world title, were held on the Tyne from time to time. Boyd won the English title and the Newcastle Chronicle Challenge Cup against W. Nicholson of Stockton-on-Tees in 1877, and was beaten by J. Higgins of Shadwell, London, in the following year. During 1878 the *Sportsman* took over the challenge cup. In 1879 Hanlan took the English title against W. Elliott of Blyth, Northumberland. In 1887 George Bubear of Hammersmith, London, beat G. Perkins of Rotherhithe, London. In 1891 W. G. East of Isleworth, Middlesex, beat G. J. Perkins of Newcastle. And in 1895 Charles 'Little Wag' Harding, the Pocket Hercules from Chelsea, London, beat the New Zealander Tom Sullivan on the Tyne.

Tynesiders made successful sorties to capture and retain these titles, notably Bob Chambers who beat

John Warkup Swift: Bob Chambers and Bob Cooper race on the Tyne, September 1864
(Tyne & Wear Archives & Museums)

Kelley from Putney to Mortlake for the world title on 29 September 1859 and defended it on the same course against Thomas White of Shadwell in 1860 and G. W. Everson of Greenwich in 1863. He lost it to Kelley in 1865, regained it against Sadler of Putney in 1866 before losing it again to Kelley on the Tyne in 1867. And Renforth brought the title back to Tyneside when he beat Kelley in 1868 from Putney to Mortlake.

Geordies would turn out in tens of thousands to watch races. The Claspers, Chambers and Renforth commanded audiences of 100,000. How these figures were assessed, of course, is anybody's guess, but what can be said with certainty is that the bridges and banks were densely crowded wherever the bookies did good business. The press gave copious coverage to important races and the crowds were knowledgeable about their sport. Further, the crowds were larger than the upstart late developer among sports, association football, could command, although the fledgling Newcastle United was eventually to become the centre of attraction for the Geordie sports fan, and the heroes of United, boosted by Cup finals and League championships early in the twentieth century, were to inherit the adulation shown to the nineteenth century scullers.

But the heyday of rowing as a popular pastime coincided with another peak of popular culture in the Tyne area—song. By the eighteenth century verbal tradition was strong among a hard working, humorous but largely illiterate population in an increasingly industrial environment. This and geographical isolation from other centres of industrial revolutionary Britain expressed itself in folk songs and topical verses that were often set to traditional tunes.

Itinerant songwriters and singers were numerous, finding audiences in public houses, music halls and private functions. They sold their latest works as pamphlets, and they did for Tynesiders what newspaper columnists, bloggers and chat shows do today. An examination of a volume of Tyne songs puts flesh and blood on the kind of purple-prosed history with which Charleton entertained us earlier. The singers put people in the streets. Allan's collection, published in 1874, covers romance and tragedy among keelmen (bargees) and fishermen, among pitmen (miners) and street eccentrics, among wherrymen and barbers who plied their trade on the quays.

The sporting heroes of the 1860s were almost all oarsmen, and their time coincided with a boom-time for many of the best writers and performers of music hall songs. Collectively, the Tyneside minstrels chronicled politics, current affairs, and incidents in local life, and they celebrated the achievements of Geordies, as often as possible at the ridicule of the men of the Thames and the south. And they were very quick to exploit a new set of circumstances, racing one another to be first out with a song.

'The late Champion Sculler, Renforth, on the Tyne' by S Hull, The Graphic, 9 September 1871 *(River & Rowing Museum)*

Ov a'yor grand rowers iv skiff or iv skull
There's nyne wi' wor Harry hes chance for to pull;
Man he sits like a duke an' he fethers se free,
Oh! Harry's the lad, Harry Clasper for me!

Haud away, Harry! Canny lad, Harry!
Harry's the king of the Tyems an' the Tyne!

He cuts through the Tyne like a fish in the sea, and the lasses all shout as he shoots by the quay, Robson continues. King of the Thames and popular with the ladies was the former miner and cinder burner, one of whose boats had been displayed at the Newcastle Polytechnic exhibition in 1848. For the Clasper testimonial in 1862, John Taylor wrote new words to a popular ballad tune that catalogued the retiring sculler's attributes: 'Plucky as ever, the still-blooming posey iv wor coaly river.' He was faultless, matchless, thoughtful. He was canny, the highest praise bestowed by a Geordie. He was wonderful, worthy and spirited. 'Yor name it will flourish when ye're gyen for iver.'

Robert 'Honest Bob' Chambers was Clasper's protégé. He gave up his work at Losh, Wilson and Bell's iron works at Walker, renowned for the strength of its labour force, where he was a puddler, stirring molten pig iron to remove impurities, to turn professional in his twenties. So like Clasper, he was from humble origins, strong, well built and with the making of a first-class oarsman, 5 feet 10 inches tall with a racing weight of 11 stone 3 lbs. Clasper exploited these attributes in his coaching and Chambers set the Tyne and Thames alight in a ten-year sparkling run, winning 89 of 101 races. In 1859 *Bell's Life* described his style as 'magnificent, and few who saw him row that latter part of race will ever forget that majestic, even, and stupendous sweep of the sculls, or the finished fall of his compact shoulders, and his back of well-defined muscles'. He won five and lost two of his world championship attempts, the first win in 1859 when he beat Harry Kelley on the Thames, and the last in 1866 when he beat Joe Sadler. Next year, aged 36, he lost the title to Kelley.

On 5 September 1864 Chambers raced Robert Cooper, the Redheugh ferryman, on the Tyne in filthy conditions. Seventeen spectator boats followed the race. Soon after the start, Chambers almost sank and found that his boat was holed. The race was declared void and run again next day in still rough conditions. Chambers won on the north station, and the painter John Warkup Swift was there to put the scene on canvas.

In 1867 Chambers was stroke of the Tyne four that won at the Paris international regatta. A year later, on 4 June in 1868, he died of tuberculosis, the endemic disease of the northeast working class. Mr. Burn, the sculptor, depicted him propped up by his right elbow on a bed of aquatic plants with an ornamental canopy over his head for his resting place in Walker cemetery. It is the largest monument in this large, crumbling, rotting Victorian burial ground not far from the Tyne, surrounded by hideous post Second World War local authority housing. The memorial was paid for by friends and admirers of Chambers who 'for a number of years upheld the honour of Tyneside as aquatic champion of England'.

Chambers naturally gained support from the songwriters, but also from southerners and amateurs in an age when professionals were held in great suspicion by gents because of the potential abuses of competing for money. 'We may say of Chambers,' said one lofty commentator almost fifty years after the untimely death, 'that apart from grand physique and science as an oarsman, he displayed qualities throughout his career which would stamp him as a model for the present day. He was always courteous, never puffed-up with success, and yet at the same time always fondly confident in his own powers and stamina. A more honourable man never sat in a boat.'

The judgment was based on an incident in 1865 on the Thames, when just before his race against Kelley, one of Kelley's friends asked Chambers if he wished to sell his boat after the match. Tyne scullers often did this to save the cost of transporting their boats home. Chambers said he would sell, and Kelley's friend, the renowned amateur Walter Bradford 'Guts' Woodgate, asked if he could try the boat after the race. 'Howay, man, try her noo, if ye like,' Chambers said, trusting a third party known to be a supporter of his opponent to set foot in his boat on the eve of the match.

Chambers's period as champion coincided with the greatest popularity of Tyneside songs. In the late 1970s, Keith Gregson conducted diligent research and found eleven Geordie songs concerned with Chambers available in modern reprints. They celebrated his victories and commiserated with his rare defeats, including this verse from George Ridley, whose most famous composition, Blaydon Races, was first delivered at Harry Clasper's testimonial dinner at Balmbras concert hall. When Chambers defeated Green, an Australian, for the world title, Ridley wrote:

> *Now lads, ye've heered of Chambers,*
> *He's bet the Asstrilyen Green,*
> *For pulling a skiff there is ne doot*
> *He's the best ther's ivor been,*
> *He has regular locomotive speed,*
> *He's upreet, honest and true*
> *Whenever he pulls wiv a pair ov sculls*
> *Aw puts on ivory screw!*

James Renforth, a former ironworker, became world champion five months after the death of Chambers when he beat Kelley on the Thames on 17 November 1868. He was backed by William Gibson, a sweep who was known throughout Newcastle as

Edward Corvan, Known as Cat Gut Jim, the Wandering Minstrel *(Corvan, a Victorian entertainer and his songs)*

Mooney. A large crowd gathered on King's Meadows in the middle of the river—long since dredged away—opposite Elswick shipyard. The *Chronicle* used pigeons trained by Billie Oxnard to fly news of the race's progress to its office. When Mooney married in St. John's Church, Westgate Road, 'his reverence' could not get in for some time because of the crowds. Afterwards at Mooney's house in Blandford Street, Renforth and the songwriter Joe Wilson put about twenty shillings' worth of coppers on a shovel, made them hot and then threw them to the crowd outside the house.

Renforth weighed 11 stone 2 pounds and stood 5 feet 7.5 inches when he shot to fame by winning the world title at the age of 26. Southern observers were not convinced of his sculling prowess, however, because Renforth duped them by faking a fast stroke using very little power when training for his match with Kelley. But after 1868 he became better known as an oarsman because, says his biographer Ian Whitehead, nobody wanted to take him on in a sculling boat.

In 1870 Renforth took part in his first trip to North America when he was included in the English champion crew who challenged the famous 'Paris crew' from St. John, New Brunswick. Renforth stroked, James Taylor, brother of the boat builder Matthew, was at bow, and Thomas Winship and John Martin were amidships.

The significance of the Paris crew was that they had turned up at the great international regatta on the Seine in 1867 pulling a heavy boat fitted with a steering contraption instead of a coxswain. They had neither straps for their feet nor buttons on their oars. They swept the board on the Seine and later in North America, and they soon caused a flutter in the European rowing world by rendering many coxswains redundant.

Several people returned from Paris with ideas. 'Guts' Woodgate of Brasenose College, Oxford, was one. In 1868 he helped to design a boat for his college that could be steered by an oarsman, and the Brasenose cox, Fred Weatherley, jumped overboard soon after his race began at Henley. His crew won by a mile, only to be disqualified, but their enterprise caused the Henley stewards to drop coxes from their four-oared events within a few years. And Jimmy Taylor went home to Newcastle and introduced coxless boats on the Tyne. In 1869 he designed a footboard-mounted steering mechanism for the pair he rowed with Renforth, enabling him to compensate when the heavier man pulled him off course.

In 1870 the Tynesiders ventured to Canada with a coxless four, and Taylor improved his mechanism to solve the problem of a fore and aft pedal inhibiting drive off the footboard. While training at Lachine—a town near Montreal originally named 'La Chine' by the French explorer Lasalle when he sailed up the St.

Yer Gannin to be a Keelman, to the tune of Jeanette and Jeanotte *(Random Rhymes)*

Lawrence thinking he was in China—Taylor designed a semi-lunar lever on a pivot that moved from side to side while allowing pressure on the board. Geordies whom he met at the works of the Canadian Grand Trunk Railway made it for him. Taylor is said to be the first man in Britain to steer a four and a pair while rowing it. On 15 September Renforth's crew, with Taylor steering the Jewitt-built *Dunston-on-Tyne* from the bow seat, easily beat the fishermen and lumberjacks of New Brunswick over six miles on the St. Lawrence. The water was so rough that many onlookers considered that the test was negated, and so the people and crew of St. John sent a further challenge to Newcastle for five hundred sovereigns a side.

During the time it took for this offer to reach Newcastle, however, the Tyne crew had broken up in acrimony. Taylor and Renforth had a series of disputes, Martin and Winship siding with Taylor, and eventually Renforth teamed up with Harry Kelley to beat Taylor and Winship in a pair-oared trial.

There was no reconciliation between Renforth, the heavyweight stroke, and Taylor the lightweight steersman who had an incredible record of wins in sculling, fours and pair-oars. The Tyne crew who went to the new course on the Kennebeccasis River, near St. John, in 1871 consisted of James Percy at bow, Robert Chambers (of Wallsend, not a reincarnation of 'Honest Bob' Chambers) at No 2, Kelley at No 3 and Renforth at stroke. They took the *England* and the *Queen Victoria* with them, using the former for practice and the latter for the race. Jewitt built both. The *Queen Victoria* was 43ft 8ins long, 7¾ins deep and 18½ins wide amidships, 6ins high at the stem and 4 at the stern, and weighed 94 pounds. A contemporary account in the *Newcastle Chronicle* describes the race on 23 August over three miles up river from Torreyburn Cove, and back again:

'The start was made, the lead was gained. But suddenly [not much more than a mile into the race] Renforth was observed to sway from side to side, and was evidently losing his mastery of the oar. Then the St. John men forged ahead and Kelley eagerly called to his mate for a spurt. But he who of old could put on spurt enough to lift his boat out of the water, could not respond to the cheery call, and with feeble utterance, he exclaimed "It's not a fit, Harry, I've had something". The oar dropped from his stricken hand, his brawny arm fell like a withered branch in a storm. Instantly all was consternation in the boat . . .'

Accounts differ as to details, this reporter saying that the boat made for the shore and tended him there, while another says that Renforth was in a collapsed state when the boat crossed the line, Kelley holding him and Percy and Chambers rowing into Appleby's wharf from where Renforth was taken to Claremont House, the crew's training headquarters. The first version is more plausible. At any rate, our reporter stated that 'cold and pulseless lay the stalwart form of the champion oarsman of England, and the dark-robed angel was standing unseen amongst the watchers to lay a spell of silence on the foam-fringed lips'. The other version has him dying in the arms of Harry Kelley, the man he had once beaten for the world sculling title.

They never found out why Renforth died. The inquest said 'over exertion'. A shock wave passed through the rowing world. The Canadians were sorrowful that the tragedy had marred the event, and they eventually named a town after the Tynesider. The sport was often unjustly criticized as being dangerous, and a death 'in action' did not help to prove its healthiness. And the news that reached Newcastle via the trans-Atlantic cable stunned the city and its waterside community. William Dunbar wrote *The Deeth o' Jimmy Renforth*:

> *He passed away in Kelley's arms as peaceful as cud be,*
> *An' then they telegraphed the news te hus across the sea;*
> *We couldn't believ'd at first, it seemed unlikely then,*
> *But it syun proved ower true, wor gallant man was gyen.*

Joe Wilson by P M Laws, Newcastle *(Tyneside Songs and Drolleries)*

'Why was losing the international boat race a great disappointment to the Renforth crew?' went the bad-punning riddle. 'Because they Percy-veered across the Atlantic, obtained suitable Chambers, everything looked Bright, and they seemed li-Kelley to win, but alas a dark cloud was ready to Renforth upon them.'

Renforth's body was brought home from New Brunswick. His friend Joe Wilson wrote three songs, one of which began:

> *Ye cruel Atlantic cable,*
> *Whay's myed ye bring such fearful news?*
> *When Tynesdie's hardly yeble*
> *Such sudden grief to bide.*
> *Hoo me heart it beats iv'rybody greets,*
> *As the whisper runs throo dowley streets*
> *We've lost poor Jimmy Renforth,*
> *The Champein O'Tyneside!*

The town went into mourning. The Newcastle and Gateshead Operatic Band led the procession on 10 September from Renforth's house in James Street, followed by the professional oarsmen and rowing club representatives from the North, followed by mutes (Winship, Martin and Robert Cooper), followed by the four-horse hearse, relatives, backers and personal friends, the Ancient Order of Freemasons, the United Order of Free Gardeners, members of other friendly societies, all walking four abreast. Thousands followed the cortège and the crowd at St. Edmund's cemetery in Gateshead was estimated at 50,000. The memorial card said 'he nobly played his part 'til death unshipped his oar'. And Mr. Burn was at work with his chisel once more for his third rowing hero in almost as many years, this time fashioning two figures, with Kelley holding Renforth in his arms. It is a striking and large memorial marking disaster on the Kennebeccasis. There are profiles of Renforth framed by a wreath on the side and back of the monument, erected by pubic subscription and, until not many years ago, visited annually by a pilgrimage of oarsmen, led by Nipper Clark, to clean it up and keep the railings smart at Christmas Handicap time. In 1992 it was restored and moved to a site outside Shipley Art Gallery in Gateshead. Renforth's oar was on display for many years at the Neville Hotel, near North Shields railway station. James Percy, the crewman, went on to become a 'penciller' for newspapers, equally at home in the boxing arena, coursing field, bowling track, cycling ground or racecourse.

Renforth's short life saw him into much more eminence than his origins would suggest. He died a freemason, and his total earnings from winning matches all over the country amounted to £2,590 in four years (Robert Coombes and Harry Clasper's lifetime purses both topped £2,000, but accumulated over 20 years). Taylor, Clasper and Jewitt became respected and their talents sought after, as we have seen, wherever boats were built in Britain. Prowess at the oar was a way up from wage slavery, a way out of ordinariness, a comfort against isolation, and it yielded considerable winnings for those at the top. Its price, like that for songwriters, was often an early death. Gregson lists other competitors as being less successful but gaining local standing, such as Winship, Bagnall, Lally, Elliott, Teesdale. In later times Phelpses and Barrys—London dynasties—competed in the Christmas Handicap.

Of the songwriters, few ignored rowing as a topic in this mid-Victorian period, and the three whom Gregson cites as most important wrote about it. They are Ned Corvan, George Ridley and Joe Wilson. Corvan was a fiddler with a Liverpool-Irish background who performed as Cat Gut Jim the Wandering Minstrel, and is best remembered for his song about a Cullercoats Fishlas. Ridley had close contact with the sporting community and a brother who was a well-known sportsman. Wilson was prolific on rowing topics and performed his own monologues. They, and a host of others such as Robson and Emery, John Kelday Smith, T. Mitchell, G. Wombwell and John Taylor chronicled the races, bolstered the heroes and concentrated Tyneside's collective conscience towards pride and confidence in keeping its end up against the main rival, London. A Newcastle sculler 'stopped the Cockneys' craw', wrote Ridley, and 'farewell the days when Lundon lads as Champions nobly shone' sang

Wilson in his *Cockney's Lament*. And the chorus of his *Bonny Boat Rower* goes:

> *For he pulls se clivor on the coally river*
> *He's myed the Cocknies glower*
> *An' he says that he'll be champion yit*
> *Maw bonny brave boat rower.*

Wilson had humour, too, witness his canny verse on the 1864 match between Robert Cooper, the 'Redheugh ferryman' whose high tempo allowed little leg use, and Robert Chambers who harnessed power and long strokes by using his legs:

> *Thor i' thor boats, a keelman cries—*
> *Aw'll back Bob for a ginney.*
> *Which Bob? Says aw, when he replies—*
> *The Bob that wins, maw hinney.*

Wilson also hinted at one of the reasons for decline of interest in rowing as the most popular sport. He revealed in a monologue that there were some people who didn't understand it, nor could see its attraction:

'Whey, Mistriss Foster,' says Joe Wilson to his oft-quoted Carlisle landlady on the occasion of a boat race, 'ye sartinly diddn't think it was a race wi' the steemboats, did ye?'

'Yis,' she says, 'aw thowt nowt else till there was anuther greet shoot "There they are." Aw diddent

Chambers and White, to the tunes of Trab, Trab or New Good Luck *(Allan's Tyneside Songs, 1862)*

knaw we was there until Foster pointed oot two men we' ne claes on, pullin for bare life on lang planks o'wood. Whey, thor wes only one man in each plank! An aw expected to see a greet lot o'cheps i'decent sized boats, an' aw cuddint help callin Foster a feul for thrawn his muney away ower such daftness, for he lost his eighteenpence, as weel as the beer, an' it started te rain agyen. An'te myek a bad job warse, we lost the train, an' if ye call that sport aw's deun wi' ye!'

The music halls declined, the songwriting diminished, the crowds dwindled for the boat racing. They sought other pastimes and other pleasures. Barge Day, the occasion when all Newcastle celebrated the place of the Tyne in its life, became a dry land event. The historian Charleton caught its mood and put it down with a tinge of purple in his history:

'The whole town turned out to see the show, and a gallant show it was. The barges of the mayor, the Trinity House and of the various trade companies, gorgeous in paint and gilding, and rowed by men in picturesque and gay costume accompanied by a flotilla of boats with streamers flying, moved away down the river amidst the firing of cannon, the ringing of bells, and the cheers of the quay. Arrived at Spar Hawk at the river's mouth, the proclamation of the jurisdiction of the corporation of Newcastle over the river was read. Then the procession returned, and sailing past Newcastle again, proceeded to the other boundary at Hedwin stream, far up the river, where the proclamation was read once more, and the rest of the day was spent in feasting and merrymaking.'

What was left of the day, anyway. The music halls have gone, but the folk song and the singers thrive in the northeast. Occasionally there is a special race off the Newcastle quays, like the Tyne versus Thames four-oared match from Spillers Mill over the half mile to Tyne Bridge in 1953 to mark the Queen's coronation, or the demonstration sculling race when the city celebrated its 900 years, attended by a crew from Renforth, New Brunswick. There's a new bridge, too—the elegant span of the Gateshead Millennium, opened in 2001.

Now the shipping has mostly left the Tyne to the seals, the rowers and the salmon. Perhaps they can reflect, the rowers that is, on how much of the songwriters' hype was once true, of how close to the truth were the versified reputations of the scullers who were portrayed invariably as honest, modest, wondrous and fair. That's not exactly what Jack Hopper thought of some whom he met round his sculling career, and Nipper Clark knew a thing or two about rogues. Cheats and vagabonds may have done their bit to stamp out interest in professional racing, but the sport, unnoticed by the spirited hard working and hard playing population, thrives on the not-so-coaly Tyne. If they should look over their shoulders from United's St. James Park (1892) or the Gateshead International Stadium (1955), the river might attract more of the best again, more of the Hoppers and Clarks.

Meanwhile, the river Tyne is still a perpetual drunkard, like the old saying says. It is always going to or from the bar. And like time, it bears many a scull.

Bibliography

R J Charleton—A History of Newcastle-on-Tyne. W H Robinson, 1885

David Clasper—Harry Clasper, Hero of the North. Gateshead: Gateshead Books, 1990

Hylton Cleaver—A History of Rowing. London: Herbert Jenkins, 1957

Sir Theodore Cook—Rowing at Henley. London: OUP, 1919

W B Coventry—The Racing Eight. Cambridge: Heffer, 1922

Peter Dillon—The Tyne Oarsmen. Newcastle upon Tyne: Keepdate, 1993

Christopher Dodd—The Story of World Rowing. London: Stanley Paul, 1992

Christopher Dodd—Water Boiling Aft, London Rowing Club 1856-2006. London: LRC, 2006

J V S Glass and J Max Patrick—The Royal Chester Rowing Club Centenary History 1839-1939. Liverpool: James Laver, 1938

Keith Gregson—Corvan, A Victorian Entertainer & His Songs. Banbury: Kemble Press, 1983

Eric Halladay—Rowing in England: a Social History. Manchester: Manchester University Press, 1990

Robert S Hunter—Rowing in Canada since 1848. Hamilton: Davis-Lisson, 1933

Thomas C Mendenhall—The Harvard-Yale Boat Race 1852-1924. Mystic: Mystic Seaport Museum, 1993

C M Pitman—Record of the University Boat Race. London: T Fisher Unwin, 1909

T H Rowland—Waters of Tyne, a river journey through history. Warkworth: Sandhill Press, 1991

Ian Whitehead—The Sporting Tyne, A history of professional rowing. Gateshead: Gateshead Council, 2002

Ian Whitehead—James Renforth of Gateshead, Champion sculler of the world, Newcastle upon Tyne: Tyne Bridge Publishing, 2004

Joe Wilson—Tyneside Songs and Drolleries. Newcastle upon Tyne: Thos. & Geo. Allan, c1890

Neil Wigglesworth—The Social History of English Rowing. London: Frank Cass, 1992

W B Woodgate—Boating. London: Longman, Green, 1888

A Historical and Descriptive View of the County of Northumberland. Mackenzie & Dent, 1811

Newspapers, periodicals and discs
Tyne sculling races featured 100 years of Hexham rowing by Jack Hopper, Hexham Courant, 26 May 1978

When the boat comes in—the songs of nineteenth century sport, K Gregson, English Dance and Song, Winter 1978

Songs of Tyneside boat racing, K Gregson, Bulletin of North East Groups for the study of Labour History, No 16, 1982

Champion Oars, songs and tunes from the Golden Age of North East Rowing 1840-1875, performed by Benny Graham, Johnny Hindle and Colin Ross, Tyne & Wear Museums

Edward Hawks aged 46, artist unknown. Hawks was an occasional member of Harry Clasper's crew *(River & Rowing Museum)*

Index

Adams, Phil, 9, 34
amateur and professional status, 3, 12, 17, 36-7, 38, 53, 54, 61-2, 69
America (schooner), 47
America's Cup, 47
Anchor pub, 11, 20
Armstrong, William, 33
    Elswick works, *13*, 24, 72
audiences/crowds, 5, 15, 61, 64, 68, 72, 84
Aylings of Putney, 50

Babcock, John, 51, 52, 53
Bagnall, Bob, *56*, 81
Balmbras concert hall, 70
Barge (Ascension) Day, *28*, 36, 46, 84-5
Barry, Bert, 11, 17
Barry rowing dynasty, 11, 16, 81
Bates, Ned, 2
Beesley, Jack, 49
betting and bookmakers, 3-5, 10, 11, 15, 17-19, 34, 36, 61, 64
Bewick, Thomas, 23
Blaydon, 11, 24
Blyth Cambois, 36
Blyth Rowing Club, *25*, *45*, *48*
boat design and construction, 34, 37-8, 39-41, 43-54
    carvel construction, 12, 37, 47
    Harry Clasper and, 37, 41-2, 43, 44, 45, 46, 47, 49-50, 52, 54-5
    coxless boats, 50, 73
    Experiment, 36
    keel-less boats, 37-8, 39, 41-2, 44, 45, 47, 50
    outriggers, 37, 44, 46-51
    sliding seats, 37, 41, 51-3, *56*
    swivel oarlocks, 37, 51
    Matthew Taylor and, 37-41, 53-4
    James Taylor and, 73-5
Bourne, Gilbert, 41
Boyd, Robert W., *22*, 62
Brasenose College, Oxford, 73
Briggs, Jack, 1, 3, 5
Bright (rower), *60*
Brown, Anthony, 46, 47
Brown, Walter, 51, 52, 61
Brown brothers (gymnasts), 9
Brownlee (rower), 15, 16
Bubear, George, 62
Bumsted, T.B., 49
Burn, George, 57, 68-9, 80

Caius College, Cambridge, 51
Calder's Brewery, 1, 9, 12
Canada, 46, 50, 51, 62, 72, 73-9, 80, 85
Carlisle, 10
Casamajor, A. A., 53
Chambers, Bill, 2, 3, 5, 15, 16
Chambers, Bob, *35*, 37, 52, 62, 67-8, 69-70
    death of (1868), 68-9
    race with Cooper (1864), *63*, 68, 82
    world title wins, 62-4, 68, 70
Chambers, Robert (of Wallsend),

60, 75, 76
Charleton, R. J., 27, 30-1, 65, 84
cheating and sabotage, 12, 14, 85
Chester-Le-Street, 11, 36
Chicago, 51
Christmas Handicap, 1, *8*, 11, *18*, *21*, 59, 80, 81
   course, 5-7, 11, 14
   draw, 3, 14
   format, 3
   handicapping system, 12-14
   Hopper in, 3, 5-6, 10, 15-19, 20
   last (1938), 7, 17
   spectators, 5, 15
   supply of boats for, 9, 12
   Thames National Rules, 14-15
Civil Engineers College, 49
Clark, John 'Nipper', 6-9, 10-11, 15, 20, 33, 80, 85
   on weightlifting, 9-10
Clasper, David, *4*, *18*, *21*
Clasper, Dorothy, 58
Clasper, Harry, *35*, 42-6, 55-6, 80
   boat design and building, 37, 41-2, 43, 44, 45, 46, 47, 49-50, 52, 54-5
   as Chambers' coach, 67, 68
   death of (1870), 55, 57-8
   Hawks family and, 33, 44, 46
   race with Coombes (1844), 41, 44-6
   race with Newell (1846), 61
   songs about, 67
   testimonial dinner (1866), 54-5, 70
Clasper, Henry, 58
Clasper, John Hawks (Jack), *35*, 41, 43, 50-1, 58
Clasper brothers, 42-3, 44, 46, 64

Collingwood, Admiral, 26
Conant, J.W., 49
Cook, Sir Theodore, *Rowing at Henley* (1919), 41, 54
Coombes, Robert, 43-4, 80
   race with Clasper (1844), 41, 44-6
Cooper, Robert, 61, *63*, 68, 79, 82
Corbridge, 23, 36
Corvan, Edward (Cat Gut Jim), *71*, 81
Countess of Coventry pub, *13*, 61
Coventry, W.B., *The Racing Eight* (1922), 39-41
Cram, Steve, 9

Dent's Hole, 46
Derwenthaugh, 42, 57
The Diamond (boat), 46
Dobson, John, 43
Dodds, Jack, 16-17
Doggett's Coat and Badge race, 11
Dublin, 47
Dunn, George, 34
Dunston, 1, 6, 11, 33, 42, 52
Dunston-on-Tyne (boat), 75
Durham, 3, 11, 26, 47, *48*
   regatta, *25*, 42-3

The Eagle (boat), 46
East, William G., 62
Ebchester, 3, 36
Elliott, W., 62, 81
Elswick, *13*, 24, 33, 72
Emmett, Frank, 46-7
Empire Club, 7, 12, 17
England (boat), 76
English, T., 16-17, 19
Eton College, 38, 46
Exeter College, Oxford, 38

Index

Experiment (boat), 36

The Five Brothers (boat), 44, 46
The Fly (boat), 46
Freeman, H.A., 52
freemasonry, 79, 80
Fulcher, H., *48*
Fulcher, J., *48*
Furnivall, Dr., 49

Gardiner, Ralph, 27
Garsfield Coke Co., 42
Gateshead, 7, 9, 17, 20, 24, 31, 33, 43
    Empire boathouse, 11-12
    International Stadium, 9, 85
    Millennium Bridge, 32, 85
    St Edmund's cemetery, 9, 80
Gibson, William (Mooney), 70-2
Golden Fleece Hotel, Blyth, *45*
Goldie, John, 52
Goodsell, Major, 17
Gosforth races, 9
Green, Richard A.W., 50-1, 70
Gregson, Keith, 70, 81
Gulston, Francis Stepney, 52

Hadrian's Wall, 2-3, 26
Halladay, Eric, *Rowing in England* (1990), 51
Hammill, James, 62
Hanlan, Ned, *22*, 62
Harding, Charles 'Little Wag', 62
Harrison, Thomas, 33
Harvard University, 50, 52
Hawks, Crawshay and Sons, Gateshead, 33
Hawks, Ned, 33, 44, 46
the Hawthorn club, 3, 5
Henley Royal Regatta, 37-8, 42, 49, 50, 52, 73

Hepple, Wilson, *13*
Hexham, 1, 5, 10, 16, 19, 23, 36
    Amateur Rowing Club, 2, 3, 5, 11, 19, 20
Higgins, J., 62
Hoare, Thomas, 35
Hopper, Isaac, 2
Hopper, Jack (Smith of Scotswood), 1-6, 10, 19, 20, 85
    in Christmas Handicap, 3, 5-6, 10, 15-19, 20
    medals and trophies, 19-20
horse racing, 9, 36
Hull, S., 66
Hunter, Bill, 1, 3, 5
Hunter, Robert S., *Rowing in Canada since 1848* (1933), 46

Jarrow, 12, 32, 42
Jewitt, Robert, 37, 41-2, 50, 52, 54, 75, 76, 80
John O'Gaunt Rowing Club, 52
Joseph Whitworth and Co., 24
The Juliette (boat), 47

Kelley, Henry, 35, *60*, 61, 75
    death of Renforth and, 76, 77, 80
    world title races, 62, 64, 68, 69, 70, 72, 77
Kendal, 10, 17
Kennebeccasis River, near St. John, 75, 76-7, 80

Lachine, near Montreal, 73-5
Lady Margaret Boat Club, Cambridge, 52
Laski Street gym, Gateshead, 9
Littledale, J.B., 41

London Rowing Club, 34, 52, 54, 81
Long, Dorman, 33-4
Lonsdale, A.P., 38
Lord Ravensworth (boat), 46
Losh, Wilson and Bell's iron works, 67

Manchester, Herbert, *Four Centuries of Sport in America* (1931), 51
Martin, John, 72, 75, 79
McKay, James, 50
Middleton (geographer), 27
Mitchell, T., 81
Mitchell, William Andrew, 29

Nassau Boat Club, New York, 51
Neville Hotel, North Shields, 80
Newburn, 24, 31
Newcastle Corporation, 27, 29, 84-5
Newcastle oar, 50
Newcastle Polytechnic, 67
Newcastle United, 15, 64, 85
Newcastle University, 24
Newcastle Upon Tyne, 24, 26-9, 31-2, 61
Newell, Robert, 47-9, 61
Nicholson, W., 62
North Shields, 29, 36, 49, 80
Northern boathouse, Gas Yard, 11
Notman, William, *60*

oar design, 50
Ord Arms Inn, Scotswood, 51
Ouseburn, 37, 41, 46
Ovingham Church, 23
Oxford and Cambridge Boat Race, 37, 38, 42, 47, 49, 52

Oxnard, Billie, 72

'Paris crew' from St. John, New Brunswick, 72-3, 75
Patterson, William, 39
Pearson, Bob, *48*
Pearson, Philip, *8*
Pearson, Pip, *48*
Percy, James, *60*, 75, 76, 80
Perkins, G., 62
Phelps rowing dynasty, 81
Pitman, C.M., *Record of the University Boat Race* (1909), 42
Pocock, William, 46
press coverage, 16, 64, 72
professional and amateur status, 3, 12, 17, 36-7, 38, 53, 54, 61-2, 69
Prudoe castle, 23

Queen Victoria (boat), 76

railways, 32-3, 61
Redheugh, 61, 68, 82
regattas, 10, *40*
    Durham, 25, 42-3
    Henley Royal, 37-8, 42, 49, 50, 52, 73
    Paris international, 68, 72-3
    prize money, 3, 34-6
    Thames, 41, 44, 46
    on Tyne, 36-7, 44
Renforth, James, 11-12, 37, 52, *60*, 66, 70-2, 80
    death of (1871), 76-80
    memorial in Gateshead East cemetery, 9, 80
    racing in New Brunswick, 72, 75-7
    James Taylor and, 61, 72,

Index

73, 75
world title wins, 64, 70, 72
Renforth, New Brunswick, 85
Rennie, John, 29
Ridley, George, 70, 81
River & Rowing Museum, Henley, 38
Robinson & Anderson brewers, 16
Royal Chester Rowing Club, 37-8, 41
Ryton, 11, 24

sabotage and cheating, 12, 14, 85
Sadler, Joseph, 61, 64, 68
Sadler, William, 51, 61
Scotswood, 11, 24, 26, 33, 42, 46, 51, 59, 61
Second World War, 7, 17
Shields, 27
Shipley Art Gallery, Gateshead, 80
Short, J., *48*
Sims, George, 54
Smith, John Kelday, 81
Somerset House, London, 24
songs, 64-7, *71*, 72, *74*, *78*, 81-4, 85
    about Chambers, 70, 82
    about Clasper, 67
    about Renforth's death, 77, 79
    Allan's collection, 65, *83*
    'Blaydon Races', 70
    'Me Bonny Brave Boat Rower', 59, 82
South Hylton, 36
South Shields, 12, 31
St Agnes (boat), 43-4
St Edmund's cemetery, Gateshead, 9, 80

St John's College, Cambridge, 49
St John's College, Oxford, 49
Steers, George, 47
Stephenson, George, 23-4
Stephenson, Robert, 33, 47
Stevens, Commodore John C., 47
Sullivan, Tom, 62
Swaddle, Thomas, 37, 54
Swift, John Warkup, *63*, 68
Sydney Harbour Bridge, 33-4
Széchenyi, Count István, 46-7

Talkin Tarn, 10, 36, 50
Taylor, James, 50, 51-2, 61, 72, 73, 75
Taylor, John, 67, 81
Taylor, Matthew, 37-41, 53-4, 72, 80
Thames, River, 11, 45, 50, 51-2, 54, 65, 67, 85
    Chambers' races on, 68, 69-70
    Clasper boats on, 41, 44, 46
    coals to, 26-7
    regattas, 41, 44, 46
Thames National Rules, 14-15
Thames Rowing Club, 52
Titania (Robert Stephenson's yacht), 47
Tollemack, Captain, 47
Tonks, T., 16
Trinity Hall, Cambridge, 49
Tunnel Inn, North Shore, 55
Tyne, River
    Barge (Ascension) Day, *28*, 36, 46, 84-5
    boat builders, 34, 37-42, 43-6, 54, 73, 75, 80-1
    boathouses, 11-12, 24
    bridges, *4*, 6, 7-9, 14, *18*, 20, *21*, 32-4, 47, 59, 85

Brown - Sadler race (1869), 51
Challenge Cup, 62
Chambers - Cooper race (1864), *63*, 68, 82
Championship course, 59
city of Newcastle and, 26-31, 84-5
Clasper - Coombes race (1844), 41, 44-6
Clasper - Newell race (1846), 61
confluence of two heads, 23
course of, 23-6
Dunston Basin, 1
English Championship races, 62
Handicap course, 5-7, 11, 14
history of rowing on, 34, 36-7, 59-62
King's Meadows Island, *13*, 36, 59-61, 72
modern day, 7, 20, 85-6
Spar Hawk, 84
Taylor Patterson race (1851), 39
tunnels, 32
upper, non-tidal, 2, 23
Willington Quay, 32
World Championship races, 22, 62, 64
see also Christmas Handicap
Tyne Amateur Rowing Club, 24, 50
Tyne Bridge, 33-4
Tynemouth, 12, 26, 27, 31

United States, 47, 50, 51, 52

Vickers, 24
Victoria (boat), 37-8

Walker and Wallsend Rowing Club, 12, 15, 16
Walker cemetery, 69
Wallsend, 15, 16, 26, 75
Warre, Edmond, 38
Weatherley, Fred, 73
weightlifting, 9-10
Wentzell and Cownden, Lambeth, 47-9
Wesley, John, 27-9
Whickham parish church, 57
White, Thomas, 64
Whitehead, Ian, 34, 72
The Sporting Tyne (2002), 55
Wilson, Joe, 72, 79, 81-4
Winship, Thomas, 52, 72, 75, 79
Winship, William, 37, 54, 81
Wolsencroft, Samuel, 49
Wombwell, G., 81
Woodgate, Walter Bradford 'Guts', 53-4, 69, 73
World Championship, 22, 37, 46, 62-4, 68, 69, 70, 72, 77
Wylam, 23-4

Yale University, 50, 52

Books by Christopher Dodd

Pieces of Eight
A book that captures the mood, personalities and tensions of the rowing scene in the last throes of the pre-Redgrave era brilliantly. It is loaded with details and secrets that are new to me.—*Sir Matthew Pinsent, four-times Olympic champion*

Water Boiling Aft (150 years of London RC)
'A captivating, beautifully produced story of energetic beginnings and Olympic success, peppered with anecdotes of redoubtable sportsmen and enriched by atmospheric illustrations. Essential for all who cheer the blades.'—*Country Life*

Battle of the Blues (with John Marks)
Magnificently illustrated, Battle of the Blues splices highlights of the first 150 Boat Races with thematic chapters by experts and Blues, including Donald Legget, Hugh Matheson, Daniel Topolski and Hugh Laurie.

The Story of World Rowing
From the Athenian trireme to halcyon days of amateurism and the Cold War age of professionalism, a wide-ranging study of manpower in boats through five continents.

Lightning Source UK Ltd.
Milton Keynes UK
UKOW03f1554310314

229160UK00001B/7/P